Roberts v. Jaycees:

WOMEN'S RIGHTS

SUPREME COURT MILESTONES

Roberts v. Jaycees:

WOMEN'S RIGHTS

SUSAN DUDLEY GOLD

Marshall Cavendish
Benchmark
New York

Marshall Cavendish Benchmark
99 White Plains Rd.
Tarrytown, NY 10591-5502
www.marshallcavendish.us

Library of Congress Cataloging-in-Publication Data

Gold, Susan Dudley.
   Roberts v. Jaycees : women's rights / by Susan Dudley Gold.
       p. cm. — (Supreme court milestones)
   Originally published under title: Roberts v. U.S. Jaycees (1984). New York:
Twenty-First Century Books, 1995.
   Includes bibliographical references and index.
   ISBN 978-0-7614-2952-4
   1. Minnesota. Dept. of Human Rights—Trials, litigation, etc.—Juvenile
literature. 2. United States Jaycees—Trials, litigation, etc.—Juvenile
literature. 3. Sex discrimination against women—Law and
legislation—United States—Juvenile literature. 4. Clubs—Law and
legislation—United States—Juvenile literature. I. Gold, Susan Dudley.
Roberts v. U.S. Jaycees (1984) II. Title.
KF228.M56G65 1999
342.7308'78—dc22

2007043021

Photo research by Connie Gardner

Cover photo by Corbis/Royalty Free

The photographs in this book are used by permission and through the courtesy of:
Ramsey County Historical Society: 6, 105; *The Granger Collection*: 40; *Library of Congress*:
12; *AP Photo*: 10, 53, 64, 67, 91, 111; *Corbis*: 1, 3; JP Laffont/Sygma, 14; Bettmann, 22,
25, 60, 72, 87; David J.and Janice L. Frent Collection, 51; *Ed Fischer*: 98; *Getty Images*:
Stock Montage, 18; Time Life, 45, 47, 83, 100; *Richard L. Varco*: 75.

Publisher: Michelle Bisson
Art Director: Anahid Hamparian
Series Designer: Sonia Chaghatzbanian

Printed in Malaysia
1 3 5 6 4 2

contents

COLLEEN O'KANE, LEFT, AND ANNE FORD NELSON STAND ON THE STEPS OF THE SUPREME COURT BUILDING IN WASHINGTON, D.C., IN 1984. THEY WERE AMONG THE WOMEN IN THE ST. PAUL, MINNESOTA, JAYCEES WHO WENT TO COURT TO FORCE THE NATIONAL ORGANIZATION TO GRANT FULL MEMBERSHIP TO WOMEN.

INTRODUCTION

ON JANUARY 1, 2001, Sydney Ward of Round Rock, Texas, took office as the national president of the Junior Chamber of Commerce. Her appointment probably was newsworthy largely because she was the first woman to hold the top post in the international business organization. Just sixteen years before, young women interested in the group could join only as associates, called Jayceettes. The club's rules barred women from becoming full members.

In the late 1970s two Minnesota chapters of the Jaycees (the club's name at the time) allowed women to be admitted as full-fledged members. The national organization claimed that the two chapters had violated the club's rules and issued orders to all state chapters not to admit women except as associates. Incensed, members of the two chapters filed a complaint with the state Department of Human Rights, charging that the club was discriminating against women in violation of Minnesota law. The state agency agreed and took the Jaycees to court.

Thus began a landmark case, *Roberts* v. *U.S. Jaycees*, that went all the way to the U.S. Supreme Court and established the right of women to equal access to private business groups. Until then, many organizations that had served as key routes to advancement for young businessmen had been closed to women. On July 3, 1984, the Supreme Court opened the club doors to all. It ruled that organizations that do business in public could not discriminate based on sex. Not even private clubs were exempt from the Court's ruling. The case was one of a long line of actions taken to protect women's rights and put women on a par with men. Businesses as well as women celebrated the decision. Northwestern Bell, in a brief filed with the Court, had argued against the Jaycees' men-only policy because it deprived the telephone company's women employees of the benefits of the club's programs and training.

The Court's ruling in the *Roberts* case helped further the cause of equal rights for women in business. Since then, many other clubs and organizations have lifted requirements that barred women members. Women's struggle for equality is not over, however. Women still earn less than men; they still face barriers to the highest-paying jobs; many still live in poverty. In the arts, sports, science, and other fields, those with prestige and power are more likely to be men. But, as seen in the *Roberts* case, gains have been made. With a new generation of leaders—both men and women—the fight for equality continues.

one
SECOND-CLASS MEMBERS

In 1975 KATHRYN EBERT was an interior architect with a firm in Minneapolis, Minnesota. A graduate of Northwestern University, Ebert was bright, young, and eager to advance in her profession. Like others in business, she decided to join the local chapter of the Jaycees, a national nonprofit group. She wanted to gain experience in public speaking and hoped to make connections with other business people in the organization.

The energetic Ebert progressed rapidly through the ranks and after a year with the Jaycees, she was chairing the chapter's training and development committee. Later in 1976 she was named to the board of directors and chaired the civic affairs committee. Next she served as vice president of the Jaycees Foundation and became a member of the executive committee. In charge of four committees, she supervised one hundred people in her volunteer work for the Jaycees. During the spring of 1977, Ebert ran for the presidency of the Minneapolis chapter. As a Jaycees member, she had been trained as a leader, becoming an effective public speaker with well-honed organizational skills. Ebert's swift climb to success in the Jaycees encouraged her employer to promote her to project team leader. In that position, she helped direct the interior design of the Pillsbury Center, a major business and financial complex being built in downtown Minneapolis.

KATHRYN EBERT, ONE OF THE ORIGINAL PLAINTIFFS IN THE CASE AGAINST THE JAYCEES, SPEAKS AT A PRESS CONFERENCE ON JULY 3, 1984, AFTER THE U.S. SUPREME COURT RULED THAT THE ORGANIZATION HAD TO OPEN ITS MEMBERSHIP TO WOMEN.

Other women, too, found that membership in the Jaycees had helped to develop their skills and had led to advancement at work. Sally Pedersen, also a member of the Minneapolis chapter, followed a company official's advice and joined the Jaycees as a way to secure a promotion. Her activities with the Jaycees, including a stint on the board of directors, propelled her into a better job at Eastman Kodak Company. During interviews for the job, she said, each company official asked about her Jaycees accomplishments.

Kathleen Hawn, a member of the Jaycees in neighboring St. Paul, Minnesota, held several top-level posts in the local and state chapters. As a district director, she oversaw three major events for the local Jaycees and received several awards for her outstanding performance. Like Ebert and Pedersen, Hawn learned through a Jaycees program how to be a successful public speaker, a skill that aided her on the job as well as in the club. She, too, attributed her promotion at work to her Jaycees achievements.

Men Only

Hawn, Pedersen, and Ebert were among the very few women accepted as full members in the Jaycees in the 1970s. For many other women, the clubhouse doors remained firmly locked. The national Jaycees headquarters, as well as most local and state chapters, allowed only men to join as members, thus able to benefit from training in public speaking and other programs. Women, usually wives of Jaycees members, could participate in an auxiliary group that worked mainly on community projects. These women had no vote in the parent organization and could not receive awards or hold office.

The Jaycees had served as a meeting place for young businessmen for years. It began in St. Louis, Missouri, in 1915 as the Young Men's Progressive Civic Association, a

MEMBERS OF THE JAYCEES AND THEIR WIVES ENJOY A BUFFET SUPPER IN 1940 IN EUFAULA, OKLAHOMA. AT THAT TIME, ONLY MEN COULD JOIN AS FULL MEMBERS OF THE CLUB. WIVES OF MEMBERS COULD PARTICIPATE IN AN AUXILIARY GROUP, THE JAYCEETTES.

local business group. Henry Giessenbier Jr., a young banker, and his friends formed the club as a place to socialize and to encourage young men to participate in public service. After changing its name to the Junior Citizens and then the Junior Chamber of Commerce (to capitalize on its connections to business and local chambers of commerce), the club went national in 1920. Its purpose was to provide young men "with [the] opportunity for personal development and achievement and an avenue for intelligent participation . . . in the affairs of their community, state and nation, and to develop true friendship and understanding among young men of all nations." It offered training programs in public speaking, business management, and leadership development and provided a forum for members to make contacts with others in the business world. Chapters also ran a number of programs to benefit local communities.

Beginning in the early 1970s, people in business began to question why the Jaycees continued as a men-only club.

The Rochester, New York, chapter opened its doors to women, only to have its charter revoked by national officials in 1972. The chapter—the second largest in the United States, with eight hundred members—sued the national organization in U.S. District Court, claiming that the Jaycees were illegally discriminating against women and that the club had improperly ejected the New York group. The suit argued that the laws that barred discrimination in public places such as restaurants and motels (termed "public accommodations" in the law) also applied to the Jaycees, a club that was open to the public. The federal court ruled in favor of the Jaycees. The ruling held that the organization did not qualify as a "public accommodation" and that the antidiscrimination laws did not apply to a private club. The U.S. Court of Appeals turned down the New York group's request to overturn the court ruling and have its charter reinstated.

In 1972 consumer advocate Ralph Nader, a former member of the club, urged the Jaycees to reject "the stale prejudices of the past and the treatment of women as ornaments." He argued that Jaycees could be key players in helping eradicate discrimination against women in the workplace. "At a time when there is much work to be done to break down barriers to women in the professional and business world," Nader wrote, "it is imperative that one of the nation's largest business organizations welcome to its membership women who can help do just that."

More calls to open Jaycees membership to both sexes followed as women entered professional careers in increasing numbers. Chapters in big cities in particular began pushing for full membership for women. These accomplished women wanted to benefit from the Jaycees' leadership training and networking opportunities. They refused to accept second-class status as associates, whose role in the club was to support the work of the men.

CONSUMER ADVOCATE RALPH NADER IN HIS WASHINGTON, D.C., OFFICE IN 1971. NADER, ONCE A MEMBER OF THE JAYCEES, CALLED ON THE ORGANIZATION TO LIFT ITS BAN ON FEMALE MEMBERS.

PILOT PROJECT

In 1975, bowing to pressure, the Jaycees national headquarters in Tulsa, Oklahoma, agreed to set up a pilot
project in three areas, allowing women in Massachusetts,
Alaska, and Washington, D.C., to join the club as full
members. Chapters in the test areas liked the experi-
ment, which brought new members to their ranks. After
three years, however, Jaycees delegates to the national
convention voted overwhelmingly to continue the ban on
women members. Many of the delegates to the June 1978
meeting came from small towns and rural areas, where
conservatives held the view that women's role should be
in the home, not the workforce.

The decision sparked controversy among the membership nationwide. At the time, 120 chapters had
admitted women as full members in their clubs. The
Jaycees' national president, Barry Kennedy, a livestock
dealer in Nebraska, pledged to revoke the charters of
Jaycees chapters that did not bar women. Kennedy
ordered that all Jaycees clubs banish women from the
membership rolls by December 1, 1978. Chicago's 370-
member chapter, headed by a woman, cut its ties with the
Jaycees after the convention vote. This officer, Joan Petra-
novich, called the national Jaycees "hypocritical." She
complained to a reporter, "Here is a group trying to help
people that spends its time trying to trip each other up."

Shortly after the December 1 deadline, members of the
Jaycees chapters in Minneapolis and St. Paul, where Ebert,
Hawn, and Pedersen were members, filed a complaint
with the Minnesota Department of Human Rights against
the national Jaycees. Their suit alleged that in barring
women from membership, the national organization was
violating the state's antidiscrimination laws.

While the complaint slowly made its way through the

TimeLine of women's rights

1860: The New York legislature passes a law to allow women to keep their property and money when they marry. Husbands no longer automatically control money their wives inherit or earn themselves.

1860: The New York legislature revises laws that gave fathers total control over their children. Before the law was passed, fathers could take offspring from their mothers and place them in the care of others.

1873: In *Bradwell* v. *Illinois* the U.S. Supreme Court upholds an Illinois law that barred women from practicing law. The high court stated that "the paramount destiny and mission of woman are to fulfill the noble and benign offices of wife and mother."

1920: The Nineteenth Amendment giving women the right to vote is ratified by the states.

1964: Title VII of the federal Civil Rights Act of 1964 bans job discrimination based on sex and prohibits sexual harassment of employees.

1975: The U.S. Supreme Court rules in *Cleveland Board of Education* v. *LaFleur* that women cannot be forced to leave the workforce after their first trimester of pregnancy.

1979: In *Duren* v. *Missouri* the U.S. Supreme Court rules that states cannot automatically exempt from jury duty women who ask not to serve.

1981: The U.S. Supreme Court, in *Kirchberg* v. *Feenstra*, strikes down a Louisiana law that gives husbands control over marital property and allows them to sell or mortgage it without spousal consent.

1984: In *Roberts* v. *Jaycees* the U.S. Supreme Court orders the organization to open membership to women.

system, Jaycees chapters in other cities defied the national organization's rule against women members. In February 1981, the Cedar Rapids, Iowa, branch of the Jaycees voted to open membership to "young persons" instead of "young men." Five women immediately joined the local group. When state and local Jaycees officials learned of the move, they took the Cedar Rapids club to federal court. The local group continued operation, but a court-ordered injunction barred the club from using the Jaycees name as long as women participated as full members. In Massachusetts, the state Jaycees organization threatened a lawsuit against national headquarters.

It became obvious that the controversy would not go away on its own. The matter would be settled—sooner or later—in the courts.

During the American Revolution, Abigail Adams lobbied her husband, John Adams, America's second president, to give women a say in the new government of the United States.

TWO
WOMEN'S RIGHT TO VOTE

THe European settlers who first arrived on American soil faced a harsh existence that could not be sustained without constant effort. Men and women worked side by side, raising crops, butchering animals, hauling wood and water, building and maintaining homes, and stoking fires. Daughters as well as sons trained as blacksmiths, printers, and workers in other trades necessary in colonial times.

As villages formed and life became more regulated, settlers turned to the English common law to govern legal affairs. Under this system, single women could own property and manage their own affairs, but married women had to turn over all control to their husbands. A woman who did not marry, however, had few options for supporting herself. Careers for women were limited. Women who did not have family money could teach or work as domestic servants, at wages much less than those paid to men. Some resorted to prostitution to survive.

Married women had no legal say in financial matters. Husbands controlled how money was spent, even if wives had inherited it or earned it. In most states a woman could not sue or be sued, could not buy or sell property without her husband's permission, and could not serve as legal guardian of her children.

SEEKING INDEPENDENCE FOR ALL

During the Revolutionary War, women shouldered much of the burden of running farms, businesses, and homes. The fight for independence inspired some to hope that women would be included in the promise of equality. Abigail Adams, who would become America's second first lady during her husband's term as president, urged that women be given a say in the new country's government. "In the new Code of Laws which I suppose it will be necessary for you to make I desire you would Remember the Ladies, and be more generous and favourable to them than your ancestors," she wrote to her husband, John Adams, then a delegate to the Continental Congress. "Do not put such unlimited power into the hands of the Husbands. Remember all Men would be tyrants if they could." She ended with a warning that if "attention is not paid to the Laidies, we are determined to foment a Rebellion, and will not hold ourselves bound by any Laws in which we have no voice, or Representation."

John Adams's reply most certainly did not please his wife. Dismissing her request as "saucy," he wrote that her "extraordinary Code of Laws" made him laugh. "Depend on it," he assured her, "We know better than to repeal our Masculine systems."

Adams was not alone in his dismissive attitude toward women. Thomas Jefferson, third president of the United States and author of the phrase "all men are created equal" in the Declaration of Independence, also rejected the notion. "Were our state a pure democracy," Jefferson wrote to a friend in 1816, "there would still be excluded from our deliberations, infants, women, . . . [and] slaves." Women, he added, could not be allowed to mix with men at public meetings because that would lead to "depravation of morals and ambiguity of issue."

Additional barriers blocked women from receiving a

good education. High schools and colleges of the time admitted only male students. Emma Willard opened the Troy Female Seminary, the country's first free high school for girls, in New York State, in 1821. Mount Holyoke Female Seminary, founded by Mary Lyon in Massachusetts, became the first institution to provide a college education for middle-income women. By 1870, women accounted for about 20 percent of resident students at American colleges and universities. The number of women seeking higher education exploded in the twentieth century with increased opportunities provided by government grants and loans. By the mid–1980s—at the time of the *Roberts* case—women earned almost half of all undergraduate college degrees, 49 percent of all master's degrees, and a third of doctoral degrees.

Antislavery Movement

During the 1800s women joined men in the battle against slavery. Many women saw similarities between their status and that of black slaves. Several of the leading feminists of the nineteenth century developed their political skills while participating in the antislavery movement. Lucy Stone, Lucretia Mott, and Elizabeth Cady Stanton, among others, attended the first national antislavery convention in New York City in 1837. Indeed, the abolition of slavery was one of the first causes regarded as sufficiently respectable to accommodate the public participation of white, upper-class women. But even within the ranks of abolitionists, women soon learned that they filled a subservient role. At the World Anti-Slavery Convention in London in 1840, Mott and Cady Stanton were not allowed to address the delegates because they were women.

The indignity led the two women to focus their attention on women's rights. On July 19 to 20, 1848, Mott and Stanton opened the Woman's Rights Convention in Seneca

LUCRETIA MOTT, CENTER, ONE OF THE ORGANIZERS OF THE FIRST WOMAN'S
RIGHTS CONVENTION AT SENECA FALLS, NEW YORK, IS PROTECTED FROM AN
ANGRY MOB OPPOSED TO THE SUFFRAGIST CAUSE.

Falls, New York. Using the Declaration of Independence as their model, the women issued their own equal rights proclamation:

> We hold these truths to be self-evident: that all men and women are created equal; that they are endowed by their Creator with certain inalienable rights; that among these are life, liberty, and the pursuit of happiness; that to secure these rights governments are instituted, deriving their just powers from the consent of the governed.

Three hundred women delegates signed the Declaration of Rights and Sentiments at the meeting. The document demanded that women be granted the right to vote, that married women be treated fairly, and that women have equal rights in legal matters. British women, a more radical group than their American counterparts, called themselves suffragettes from the word *suffrage*, meaning the right to vote. American women who lobbied for the vote became known as suffragists.

Susan B. Anthony first met her mentor, Cady Stanton, at one of the women's rights conventions held over the next thirteen years in the East and Midwest. The two feminists became partners in the fight for women's equality. Like many other advocates for women's rights, Anthony and Cady Stanton joined the temperance movement, the campaign to ban alcohol. They believed that alcohol abuse led husbands to strike their wives. Once again, however, the women activists learned that male advocates did not value their opinions. At a meeting of the Sons of Temperance in 1851, Anthony rose to offer a resolution as a representative of the Rochester Daughters of Temperance. The male moderator quickly told her to sit down. "The sisters were not invited here to speak, but to listen and learn!" he told a fuming Anthony. Irate, she and Cady Stanton marched out. They later formed their own temperance organization, the Woman's New York State Temperance Society, which attracted 20,000 members.

By the mid–1800s women activists had made some progress. In 1849 Elizabeth Blackwell became the first woman doctor in America, graduating first in her class at Geneva Medical College in New York State. After studying further in Paris, she practiced at St. Bartholomew's Hospital in London. When she returned to the United States, male doctors refused to work with her and hospitals would not employ her. So she set up her own practice and in 1857 opened the New York Infirmary for Women and Children with her sister Emily, also a doctor. Blackwell later established medical schools for women in the United States and London.

Women broke down barriers in business, law, and other fields. In 1866 Lucy Hobbs graduated from dental school, the first American woman to do so. Arabella Mansfield became the nation's first woman lawyer, in 1869, followed fifteen years later by Ada H. Kepley, who was the first woman to graduate from law school. Women made gains in politics as well. Even without the right to vote in presidential elections, women began to serve in various posts on the local level. In 1887 citizens of Argonia, Kansas, elected Susanna Medora Salter as the first woman mayor of a U.S. municipality.

Frederick Douglass, the foremost black civil rights leader of the day, supported the women's campaign for equal rights. Most male leaders, however, fiercely opposed the women's rights movement. They contended that the rough-and-tumble worlds of politics and business were unsuitable for delicate women, who needed male protection. Laws in several states reinforced that contention. In New York, for example, laws gave men control over all the

SUSAN B. ANTHONY (STANDING) AND ELIZABETH CADY STANTON READ A LETTER TOGETHER. THE TWO WOMEN WERE LEADERS IN THE CAMPAIGN FOR WOMEN'S RIGHTS IN THE NINETEENTH CENTURY.

family finances, including money women had acquired before marriage. Men could transfer custody of their children to someone other than their mother or send them to the poor house if they chose to do that.

Cady Stanton unmasked such laws for what they were— a way to keep women under control and dependent on men. The laws, she argued, robbed women of the right to run their own lives. In March 1860 Cady Stanton delivered a speech to the state legislature in New York, urging passage of a law ensuring the rights of married women. Titled "A Slave's Appeal," her speech moved the lawmakers to approve the measures.

Cady Stanton told legislators to "let us take care of ourselves, our property, our children and our homes." Women, she said, did not want or expect men to take care of them: protection was a poor trade for loss of control over one's own life. The feminist leader noted that women, like men, had "the necessary powers for self-support, self-defence and protection." She urged the lawmakers to "undo what man did for us in the dark ages, and strike out all special legislation for us." Women, she continued, should not be a separate category in state constitutions but should stand equal to men. Her stirring plea to "Let us sink or swim, live or die, survive or perish together" brought applause and passage of the legislation. The new law granted married women the right to keep the money they earned, to file suits in court, to make contracts, and to have joint custody of their children.

Two years later, however, the legislature amended the law, denying widows automatic custody of their children and control of their children's property. The partial turnabout represented the path women were to travel to win equal rights: a seesaw route of gains and losses over many years.

BLACK MEN—BUT NOT WOMEN—WIN VOTE

On January 1, 1863, President Abraham Lincoln signed the Emancipation Proclamation freeing slaves in the South. Abolitionists—those working to end all slavery—continued the push to stop the practice throughout the nation. During the Civil War, Anthony and Cady Stanton collected the signatures of 400,000 supporters of full citizenship for slaves in the North and for women. Their efforts helped pass the Thirteenth Amendment, which abolished slavery in the United States. They continued to work for passage of the Fourteenth Amendment, which they believed would grant both women and former slaves the right to vote. However, men lobbying for voting rights for blacks argued that including women in the amendment would jeopardize its chances of passage. For an amendment to be enacted, it must first win approval from two-thirds of Congress, then be passed by three-quarters of the state legislatures.

The final wording of the Fourteenth Amendment states that "all persons born or naturalized in the United States" were to be considered citizens. It prohibits states from abridging "the privileges or immunities of citizens." The amendment also declares that states were to be penalized if they denied the vote to "male inhabitants." Until that time, the Constitution had not referred to male and female citizens, only to "mankind" or "man," words that could be assumed to include women and well as men. The word *male*, however, specifically excludes women. Enraged, Cady Stanton and Anthony withdrew their support of the amendment—after having worked for years to win its passage. The amendment was ratified on July 28, 1868, with the vote of the twenty-eighth state, South Carolina.

Feminists tried again to persuade Congress to grant women the right to vote by means of the Fifteenth Amendment, but their efforts failed. Ultimately, the amendment barred states from denying the right to vote on the basis of race or color only. Speaking for women's rights, Anthony told Congress, "I would sooner cut off my right hand than ask for the ballot for the black man and not for woman."

On March 15, 1869, Congressman George W. Julian from Indiana proposed a constitutional amendment to grant women the right to vote. His colleagues ignored the bill, which Julian had introduced at the request of Cady Stanton and Anthony. Opponents argued that allowing women to vote would cause upheaval in society, destroy families, and undermine the church and the government. Over the next fifty years, similar amendments would be proposed only to be shot down by Congress. Anthony lobbied for women's voting rights before every Congress from 1869 until 1904. Stanton, an accomplished writer whose work appeared in numerous newspapers, authored the position papers presented by the group to Congress and state legislatures. "She forged the thunderbolts and I fired them," Anthony said of their collaboration. Neither would live to see women win the right to vote.

women Lose in court

More discouraging news for supporters of women's rights came in 1872, when the U.S. Supreme Court denied a young woman's petition to practice law. The case, *Bradwell v. Illinois*, involved a married woman, Myra Bradwell, who had passed the Illinois bar exam and met all that state's qualifications to practice law. Nevertheless, the Illinois Supreme Court prevented her from practicing law because she was a woman. Bradwell claimed that the ruling infringed on her rights as a citizen, which the Fourteenth Amendment protected. In an 8 to 1 decision, the U.S. Supreme Court upheld the lower court's ruling. According to the Court, states had the right to establish their own rules for admission to the bar. The ruling limited the

protections offered by the Fourteenth Amendment, especially when it came to women. Justice Joseph P. Bradley,
who agreed with the ruling, issued a separate opinion in
which he stated the stereotypical view of women as unfit to
pursue a career outside the home:

> Man is, or should be, woman's protector and
> defender. The natural and proper timidity and del-
> icacy which belongs to the female sex evidently
> unfits it for many of the occupations of civil life. . . .
> One [maxim of law] is, that a married woman is
> incapable, without her husband's consent, of
> making contracts which shall be binding on her or
> him. This very incapacity was one circumstance
> which the Supreme Court of Illinois deemed impor-
> tant in rendering a married woman incompetent
> fully to perform the duties and trusts that belong to
> the office of an attorney and counsellor. . . . The
> paramount destiny and mission of woman are to
> fulfil the noble and benign offices of wife and
> mother. This is the law of the Creator.

In 1875 another case, *Minor* v. *Happersett*, reinforced
the Court's refusal to extend Fourteenth Amendment protections to women's rights. The petitioner, Virginia
Minor, argued that the amendment protected her right as
a citizen to vote. The Court rejected her plea, stating in its
unanimous decision that states had the right to decide who
could vote.

PUSHING FOR THE VOTE

Suffragists continued their efforts to win a hearing for
their cause. In 1877 Susan B. Anthony presented Congress
with petitions signed by more than 10,000 people from
twenty-six states in support of women's right to vote. As

susan b. anthony amendment (amendment xix)

Section 1. The right of citizens of the United States to vote shall not be denied or abridged by the United States or by any State on account of sex.

Section 2. Congress shall have power, by appropriate legislation, to enforce the provisions of this article.

they had in the past, members of Congress ignored the demands. Anthony's ceaseless campaign finally forced the Senate in 1887 to vote on a proposed amendment named in her honor. Only fifty of the Senate's seventy-six members, however, chose to appear for the vote, which rejected the Susan B. Anthony Amendment 34 to 16. Anthony addressed Congress on the issue for the last time in 1904, two years before her death. "We have waited. We stood aside for the Negro, we waited for the millions of immigrants. . . . How long," she asked, "will this injustice, this outrage, continue?"

Despite consistent opposition from Congress, women had already cast ballots in elections in many areas, especially in the West. Wyoming women voted in all elections after the territory became a state in 1869. Women in Utah did the same in 1870, and Colorado and Idaho gave women full voting rights in the 1890s. Many states permitted women to vote in local elections but not national races.

After Anthony died in 1906, other women took her place to continue the fight. Carrie Chapman Cott led moderates in the battle. They lobbied every state legislature to change the voting laws on the local level. Suffragist Alice Paul and members of the National Woman's Party marched down Pennsylvania Avenue in front of the White House in 1913. They demanded that President Woodrow Wilson support their cause. Another demonstration in 1915, on Fifth Avenue in New York City, drew further attention to the issue. The measure failed to pass the House of Representatives by seventy-eight votes that year. Paul continued to push for passage, leading women in hunger strikes and picket lines.

America's entry into World War I in 1917 helped carry the suffragist movement to victory. During the war, women took on the jobs men had left behind when they became soldiers. This demonstration of women's abilities pushed politicians, including President Wilson and some members of Congress, to back the suffragists' demands. When the Susan B. Anthony Amendment was again introduced in the House of Representatives on January 10, 1918, the president urged Congress to pass it. Although the House passed the amendment with one vote more than necessary, the measure lost by two votes in the Senate.

But the momentum was building. Sixteen states had already granted women full voting rights, and fourteen other states allowed them to vote in presidential elections. On May 21, 1919, the House approved women's suffrage by a fourteen-vote margin over the required two-thirds vote. The Senate continued to fight the inevitable. After losing by one vote in the Senate on February 10, 1919, supporters of women's voting rights resubmitted the bill and led a public relations campaign to pressure senators to pass the amendment. Southern Democrats staged a brief filibuster but soon abandoned the effort when it became apparent they would lose. They had argued that each state should have the right to determine which of its residents qualified as voters. The South had used much the same arguments in taking a stand against granting black citizens the right to vote in the 1800s.

Finally, after four hours of debate—and a battle that began with the American Revolution—the Senate adopted the Susan B. Anthony Amendment on June 4, 1919, by a vote of 56 to 25, two more than the two-thirds majority needed. Supporters in the Senate galleries greeted the announcement of the final vote with "deafening applause."

RATIFICATION—STATE BY STATE

Suffragists immediately announced they would push for states to convene special sessions to vote on the amendment so that women would be able to cast their ballots in the next presidential election, in November 1920. Legislatures in three-quarters of the states had to approve the measure before it could become national law.

Five states ratified the amendment within days. Illinois became the first, on June 10, 1919. That state's Senate voted unanimously to back the amendment; only three House members opposed it. Later the same day, legislatures in both Wisconsin and Michigan approved the measure. Kansas and Ohio voted for women's suffrage six days later.

New York became the sixth state to ratify the amendment. In an "extraordinary" late-night session on June 16, the state legislature approved the measure without one dissenting vote. During debate on the issue, Socialist leader August Claessens declared that women "want a voice in the industrial life of this nation, and you won't have a democracy until that right is granted them."

Other states followed the lead of the first six states. By the end of 1919, twenty-two states had ratified the amendment. Many states in the South, however, rejected the amendment or refused to vote on it. Georgia, Alabama, South Carolina, Virginia, Maryland, Mississippi, and Louisiana all voted to reject the measure. In response to a June 11, 1919, editorial in the *New York Times*, a letter writer from Alabama dismissed the prediction that his state would ratify the amendment any time soon. He asserted that the women of his state, "true to the traditions of the South," did not want the right to vote. "Why should it be thrust upon them?" he asked. Alabama residents, he noted, "both white and colored," favored the status quo (that barred women from voting). He warned that black voters would take over control of half the South if women, in particular black women, won the right to vote. Alabama, he vowed, would not expose its women "to the dangers and humiliation that would follow the adoption of the Anthony amendment." Southerners feared that passage of the voting rights act for women would reopen examination of the South's registration of voters. Many areas of the South enforced registration requirements that prevented black men from voting.

The measure did not reach the required three-quarter mark for nearly nine months. Ironically, a southern state would be the one to provide the final vote needed for the amendment to become law. On August 18, 1920, Tennessee became the thirty-sixth state to ratify Amendment XIX on a close vote of 50 to 46. That action, after a fifty-year campaign, gave U.S. women the right to vote, with time to spare before the presidential election in November.

Though their votes were no longer necessary, two more states—Connecticut and Vermont—ratified the measure in September and February 1921. Delaware, which had voted against women's suffrage earlier, added

LIsten to your MoTHer

On August 18, 1920, members of the Tennessee House ratified the Susan B. Anthony Amendment granting women the right to vote. With that action, Tennessee became the final state needed for formal ratification of the measure. The state senate had already passed a resolution approving the amendment.

The House vote—50 to 46—almost went the other way. With two days left in the session, the Speaker, Seth Walker, proposed tabling the matter. Ninety-six of ninety-nine members present cast a tie vote on Walker's motion, which was confirmed by a second vote. Opponents of women's suffrage immediately asked for a roll call vote on the amendment itself. They expected all those who had cast their ballots for Walker's motion to vote against the amendment. A tie vote would have meant defeat for the suffrage side.

Spectators on both sides of the issue packed the room. Suffragists wore yellow roses in their lapels, while those opposed to the amendment sported red roses.

As the chair called for each member's vote, tension rose in the chamber. Hundreds of suffragists, on hand for the event, believed the cause was lost. Then Representative Harry T. Burn, a Republican and at twenty-two the youngest member of the body, voted in favor of the measure. He had previously voted to table the measure, and his vote this time tipped the balance to the suffragists. But then Representative B. P. Turner, a Democrat, declined to vote, as he had said he would do. Antisuffragists gave shouts of joy. Turner had voted against tabling the earlier motion, so the advantage slipped once again to those opposed to suffrage. Stunned suffragists feared the amendment would go down in defeat.

Emotions ran high as each member in turn cast his vote. Just as the roll call neared an end, Turner, who had abstained from voting earlier, announced that he had decided to vote for the amendment, thus assuring victory for amendment supporters. Pandemonium broke out as the suffragists cheered wildly. The *New York Times* described the scene this way:

> The suffragists launched an uproarious demonstration before the clerk announced the vote, for there was no question that they had won. Women screamed frantically. Scores threw their arms around the necks of those nearest them and danced, so far as it was possible to do so, in the mass of humanity. Hundreds of suffrage banners were waved wildly, and many removed the yellow flowers they had been wearing and threw them upward to meet a similar shower from the galleries.

Angry opponents of the amendment ran after the man whose vote gave the suffragists the advantage, Representative Burn. He managed to hide in the Capitol's attic to escape harm. Burn, who had worn the red rose symbol of the antisuffragists in his lapel, later explained that he had changed his vote because of a letter from his mother. In the letter, which he carried in his pocket during the vote, Febb Ensminger Burn told her son that she had been watching him to see how he stood on women's voting rights. "Hurrah, and vote for suffrage!" she wrote. "Don't keep them in doubt." In the House the next day, Burn said he voted the way he did because he believed every citizen had a right to vote, that the legislator had "a moral and legal right to ratify," and that "a mother's advice is always safest for her boy to follow."

its ratification in 1923. The remaining southern states would not give their approval until many years later. Maryland voted for ratification in 1941, though its vote was not certified until 1958; Virginia and Alabama added their support in the early 1950s. Legislators in Florida and South Carolina approved the measure in 1969, followed by Georgia and Louisiana in 1970 and North Carolina in 1971. Finally, in 1984, Mississippi—the last of the forty-eight states in existence when the amendment became law—formally voted to ratify women's right to vote.

THree
AN AMENDMENT FOR
EQUAL RIGHTS

THe suffraGISTS HaD envisioneD that win-
ning the vote would be the key women would use to open
doors to opportunity in other areas of their lives. Though
women rejoiced at finally having the right to vote, they
soon realized that the end of that battle marked the
beginning of the next.

During a conference marking the seventy-fifth
anniversary of the first Woman's Rights Convention at
Seneca Falls, the National Woman's Party (NWP) drew up
a proposed amendment to the Constitution that would
grant equality to women. Authored by NWP vice president
and longtime suffragist Alice Paul, the amendment read:
"Men and women shall have equal rights throughout the
United States and every place subject to its jurisdiction."
President Calvin Coolidge met with a delegation of
women and assured them that he did not have "the
slightest doubt that Congress will respond favorably" to
the measure.

At Paul's urging, Representative Daniel Anthony,
nephew of Susan B. Anthony, introduced the first equal
rights amendment (ERA) to Congress in 1923. Despite the
president's assurances, however, the nation's lawmakers
showed little interest in or support for the proposal.
Opponents prevented it from getting a hearing, and it

remained in committee in both the House and the Senate for the next twenty-three years.

At first several prominent mainstream women's groups opposed the ERA. The League of Women Voters, the National Consumers League, and the Women's Trade Union League all worked for women's causes but took stands against the amendment. Chief among the reasons for their opposition was the fear that the amendment would wipe out labor laws that specifically protected women from long hours and unhealthy workplace conditions. The U.S. Supreme Court upheld such laws in *Muller v. Oregon*, a 1908 case that addressed Oregon's law limiting the number of hours women could work. State lawmakers had originally passed the law to protect women from conditions they believed might harm their ability to have children. Justice David J. Brewer wrote in the Court's majority opinion that:

> woman's physical structure and the performance of maternal functions place her at a disadvantage in the struggle for subsistence . . . the physical well-being of women becomes an object of public interest and care in order to preserve the strength and vigor of the [human] race.

The decision set the stage for many more such laws that treated men and women differently. By 1925, eighteen states required rest periods and lunch breaks for women (but not men). Women were not allowed to work at night at certain jobs in sixteen states. Many women praised these laws, but Paul and her supporters believed such restrictions limited the number of jobs open to women and made it harder for them to succeed in the business world.

The argument for protective labor laws for women lost some of its steam when Congress passed the Fair Labor

Standards Act in 1938. The act established a minimum wage, set requirements for overtime pay, and limited the number of hours for male and female workers. It also put severe restrictions on labor by children. With the law's passage, ERA supporters argued, separate laws to protect women were no longer necessary. Opponents of the ERA, however, insisted that women and men should be treated differently. In their view, women's primary role was to maintain the home and care for the children; those who did work outside the home were believed to need extra protection because women were weaker than men.

Rosie the Riveter

World War II dramatically changed the way Americans viewed women's work. With millions of men away at war, the nation depended on women to fill jobs once held exclusively by men. The government launched a full-scale advertising campaign to recruit women workers, many of whom had never worked outside the home. J. Howard Miller, an artist employed by Westinghouse, created the image of a woman flexing her muscle and proclaiming "We Can Do It!" Miller's drawing was soon linked with a popular song of the 1940s, "Rosie the Riveter," by Redd Evans and John Jacob Loeb. Rosie soon began appearing on posters and in other media of the time.

The well-known illustrator Norman Rockwell depicted Rosie as a robust woman with muscular arms, wearing overalls and safety goggles, and cradling a riveting gun. This Rosie (with the U.S. flag in the background) is all-American and ready to work to defeat the enemy (symbolized by the copy of *Mein Kampf*, the infamous autobiography of German dictator Adolf Hitler, beneath her feet). Rosie's face and hands are dirty, but lipstick, rouge, and nail polish assert her femininity. The image graced the cover of the May 29, 1943, issue of the *Saturday Evening Post*, a

THIS CARTOON PUBLISHED IN THE 1940S WAS A COMMENTARY ON THE GROWING
NUMBER OF WOMEN ENTERING THE WORKFORCE DURING WORLD WAR II.

magazine read by millions. Newspapers, magazines, films, radio stations, and stores all portrayed women at work, featuring Rosie as well as real-life women on the job. The message that working outside the home was not only acceptable for women but also their patriotic duty helped persuade millions of women to apply for wartime jobs. The effort proved to be the most successful advertising recruitment campaign in U.S. history.

First Lady Eleanor Roosevelt also provided a strong role model for women. As one of President Franklin D. Roosevelt's chief advisers, she carved out her own role as an advocate for the poor and the disadvantaged. She toured the country, wrote a daily newspaper column, held press conferences, and gave lectures. After the war, she served as the U.S. delegate to the United Nations and chaired the commission that drafted the Universal Declaration of Human Rights, adopted by the international organization in 1948.

At the height of the war, more than 19 million women joined the workforce. Poor women, forced by their circumstances to work, had always held paying jobs. Many of these jobs, however, were considered "women's work," in low-wage service industries such as laundries and textile and shoe factories. The war gave many poor women the opportunity to work at more skilled jobs for much higher wages. They were joined by about 6 million women who had never before worked outside the home. These new workers were often white, middle-class, married women.

For members of both groups, the war jobs were a life changing experience. Being employed gave women a sense of worth and a way to achieve independence. While many women left jobs to resume life as full-time housewives and mothers after the war, others kept their place in the workforce. One wartime worker, Sybil Lewis, a riveter at aircraft manufacturer Lockheed, said, "You came out to

California, put on your pants, and took your lunch pail to a man's job. This was the beginning of women's feeling that they could do something more." Another, Inez Sauer, who worked as a tool clerk in the same industry, expressed similar sentiments. She said that "at Boeing I found a freedom and an independence that I had never known. After the war I could never go back to playing bridge again, being a club woman . . . when I knew there were things you could use your mind for. The war changed my life completely."

DEMANDING EQUAL RIGHTS

Now that women had proven their worth at the job site, they wanted equal treatment at work and in other areas of their lives. Buoyed by the nation's gratitude for women workers' contributions to the war effort, activists led by the illustrious Alice Paul pushed once again for passage of the ERA. Revised in 1943, the proposed amendment's new wording proclaimed: "Equality of rights under the law shall not be denied or abridged by the United States or by any State on account of sex."

Although the ERA had been introduced in Congress every year for twenty-three years, the lawmakers had never voted on the amendment. In 1946 the Senate agreed to vote on the issue. As in the past, women's groups split over the issue. About half the organizations took a pro-ERA stand; the others claimed that the amendment would expose women workers to harsher conditions. Governors, too, split about evenly on the amendment.

Opponents in the Senate, many of them Democrats from the South, contended that the ERA would give the federal government control over matters such as marriage, property rights, and children that had always been the domain of individual states. Speaking in favor of the amendment, however, Democratic senator J. F. Guffey of Pennsylvania called the ERA a "step forward like the suffrage amendment." He noted that early suffragists had issued their declaration of rights in 1848 and urged fellow senators to send the amendment on to the states. "One hundred years should be enough to fight for justice," he said. Other northern Democrats, however, sided with the labor unions and took a stand against the measure. The unions, which generally backed Democratic candidates, feared that passage of the ERA would allow women to take jobs from their male members.

ERA proponents won a major advantage when President Harry S. Truman expressed support for the bill. A majority of the senators voting approved the amendment 38 to 35. In the end, however, the amendment failed to obtain the required two-thirds vote needed to send it to the states for ratification. Twice as many Democrats as Republicans voted against the amendment. Both political parties, however, had endorsed the ERA in their platforms.

Dorothy Smith McAllister, leader of the National Consumers League, which was active in the fight to protect women workers, cheered the defeat of the ERA. "Fifty years of labor legislation to meet the special needs of women in industry has been saved by the vote today," she told the *New York Times*. Nevertheless, Alice Paul expressed optimism that the vote indicated growing support for the amendment and predicted that the Senate would eventually pass the measure.

In 1950 and again in 1953 the Senate voted for the ERA, but only after adding a rider that essentially canceled any protection of women's rights. The rider, proposed by Democrat Carl Hayden of Arizona, read: "The provisions of this article shall not be construed to impair any rights, benefits, or exemptions now or hereafter conferred by law upon persons of the female sex." It was not even considered in the House, where Judiciary Committee chairman Emanuel Celler, a Democrat from New York who strongly opposed the ERA, continually blocked the amendment from coming to the floor.

Proponents continued their campaign to preserve the amendment and presented it to Congress every year without success. In 1963 Betty Friedan's book *The Feminine Mystique* drew attention to the plight of women and their unequal status in American society. Finally, in 1970, U.S. Representative Martha Griffiths, a Democrat from Michigan and the first woman to win a seat on the House Ways and Means Committee, filed a petition to override the Judiciary Committee and bring the ERA to the full House for a hearing. Representatives passed the petition and the amendment. But the Senate's demand that exemptions be added to the ERA killed its chances for final passage.

During the next session, the House approved a new version of the amendment giving Congress the power to enforce its provisions, which were to become effective two years after ratification. The compromise wording also set a seven-year deadline: if the amendment had not been ratified by then, it would be withdrawn from the process. The House passed the revised amendment on October 12, 1971.

In the Senate, Democrat Sam J. Ervin Jr. of North Carolina proposed seven amendments to limit the ERA's scope. He argued that Congress should keep in place all laws that exempted or protected women. He also sought to exempt women from combat and from the draft. Senators rejected all of Ervin's proposals. After the failure of Ervin's attempts to dilute the amendment, the Senate voted overwhelming approval for the measure. Only eight senators, two Democrats and six Republicans, opposed the amendment. The scene in the gallery was reminiscent of the jubilation of suffragists when the Senate approved the Nineteenth Amendment in 1919. Women of all ages and men who supported the ERA "applauded, cheered and let out a few cowboy yells," according to a newspaper account of the vote.

U.S. REPRESENTATIVE MARTHA W. GRIFFITHS, THE FIRST WOMAN TO SERVE ON THE HOUSE WAYS AND MEANS COMMITTEE, PICTURED HERE IN 1962, PLAYED A LEAD ROLE IN THE CAMPAIGN TO WIN PASSAGE FOR THE EQUAL RIGHTS AMENDMENT.

THE EQUAL RIGHTS AMENDMENT, PASSED BY CONGRESS IN 1972

Section 1. Equality of rights under the law shall not be denied or abridged by the United States or by any State on account of sex.

Section 2. The Congress shall have the power to enforce, by appropriate legislation, the provisions of this article.

Section 3. This amendment shall take effect two years after the date of ratification.

FIGHT FOR RATIFICATION

Proponents predicted a swift ratification by the states. Hawaii became the first to ratify; its House and Senate voted for the amendment only thirty-two minutes after the U.S. Senate approved the measure.

By 1976, as the nation paused to celebrate the bicentennial of its independence, thirty-four states had ratified the ERA. Support from other states came harder. Opponents led by Phyllis Schlafly, a conservative Illinois Republican, ran a well-financed national campaign against ratification. Among other tactics, they raised the specter of women forced to share men's bathrooms, girls being drafted (even though the draft had been eliminated), and mothers losing custody of their children.

Indiana became the thirty-fifth state to ratify the ERA in 1977. There the effort to win final ratification for the amendment stalled. As the seven-year deadline neared

PHYLLIS SCHLAFLY, A VOCAL OPPONENT OF THE EQUAL RIGHTS AMENDMENT, SPEAKS TO A CROWD GATHERED AT THE STATE CAPITOL IN SPRINGFIELD, ILLINOIS, IN MARCH 1975.

without the required approval of thirty-eight states, ERA proponents, led by the newly organized National Organization for Women (NOW), asked Congress to extend the time. They won a three-year reprieve, but it turned out to be a case of too little too late. With constant pressure from anti-ERA forces, the tide began to turn. Ronald Reagan, elected in 1980, opposed the amendment, the first president to do so. Some states that had previously ratified the ERA took steps to rescind their approval.

On June 30, 1982, fifty-nine years after the first ERA was introduced to Congress and three votes short, the proposed Twenty-seventh Amendment to the Constitution went down in defeat. The struggle to pass the ERA, however, focused the nation's attention on the issue of women's rights. In the courts, in Congress, in state legislatures, and in the workplace, more and more women began to demand equal treatment.

four
OPENING CLOSED DOORS

An amendment to the constitution did not offer the only hope of equality for women. Various groups began organizing to push for women's equal rights through court actions, through state legislation, and in other venues.

Anne R. Davidow of Michigan was the first attorney to argue before the U.S. Supreme Court that the Fourteenth Amendment offered equal protection to women as well as men. In the 1948 case of *Goesaert* v. *Cleary*, Davidow represented a woman who owned a bar in Michigan and wanted to hire her daughter as a bartender. State law prohibited women from tending bar unless the business was owned by their husband or their father. Under the law, however, women could do lower-paying waitress work. Davidow argued that the Michigan statute should be struck down because the Fourteenth Amendment's equal protection clause extended to women being discriminated against by state laws. The Court ruled otherwise. In its decision, the justices concluded that Michigan lawmakers had rightfully sought to protect women through "rational social legislation." Although Davidow lost in court, at her urging the Michigan legislature later repealed the law.

By the late 1940s and early 1950s, soldiers returning from World War II had reclaimed their jobs and women

fourteenth amendment, section 1

All persons born or naturalized in the United States and subject to the jurisdiction thereof, are citizens of the United States and of the State wherein they reside. No State shall make or enforce any law which shall abridge the privileges or immunities of citizens of the United States; nor shall any State deprive any person of life, liberty, or property, without due process of law; nor deny to any person within its jurisdiction the equal protection of the laws.

had been relegated to more traditional types of employment: lower-paying jobs in the labor force and work at home for no pay. Betty Friedan, who would became a leader in the fight for women's rights, lost her job as a newspaper reporter when a veteran claimed it. Among her scoops had been a wartime interview with Eleanor Roosevelt and a report on a major transit strike. She later worked for a labor union newspaper but lost that job as well when she became pregnant.

Although many women left the workforce after the war to raise families, the number of female workers never returned to prewar levels. In the 1950s and 1960s women continued to seek careers outside the home. Almost 60 percent of new workers in the 1950s were women. By 1960, women accounted for one-third of the workforce. Most held the lowest-paying jobs.

Several factors led to the increase in women on the job. Many female wartime workers had experienced for

BUTTONS USED TO PROMOTE THE CAUSE OF EQUAL PAY FOR WOMEN. WHEN PRESIDENT JOHN F. KENNEDY SIGNED THE EQUAL PAY ACT IN 1963, WOMEN EARNED FIFTY-NINE CENTS FOR EVERY DOLLAR A MAN RECEIVED. WOMEN CAMPAIGNING FOR THE PASSAGE OF THE EQUAL RIGHTS AMENDMENT IN THE 1970S WORE THE BUTTONS AS A SIGN THAT WOMEN CONTINUED TO EARN LESS THAN THEIR MALE COUNTERPARTS.

the first time the satisfaction of being paid for a job well done. Women were living longer and having fewer children, leaving them with more time to pursue a career. Even mothers of young children began looking at employment as a way to help with rising costs as people sought to better their lives. Many families bought homes and cars, as well as an increasing number of consumer goods. The rising divorce rate was another factor. Single mothers found themselves forced into the labor market to support themselves and their children.

With the growing numbers of women in the workforce, activists stepped up efforts to end discrimination and to open jobs and careers to people of both sexes. In 1965 Congress passed the Equal Pay Act, the first federal law to prohibit private businesses from discriminating against women. Originally proposed in 1945, the law required employers to give equal pay to men and women doing the same job. The statute excluded several major categories of employment, however, including teaching and administrative and executive posts.

Even with the law in place, women continued to face discrimination on the job. They had little chance of winning executive and management positions, nor did they get more than token consideration for the more traditional male jobs in construction and similar work. Women had to meet rigid requirements even in jobs held exclusively by women. Almost all the flight attendants (then called stewardesses) hired by the airlines had to be female, young, attractive, single, and white. When the stewardesses reached their thirties or married, they lost their jobs.

TITLE VII: Landmark Legislation

Women working to change the system sought help from Congress. As the suffragists had once sought to be included in legislation designed to give African Americans the right to vote, activists for women's rights asked that women be included in the Civil Rights Act of 1964. This time they had better results.

As the centerpiece of President Lyndon B. Johnson's efforts to ensure the rights of African Americans, the Civil Rights Act of 1964 dealt with employment, housing, access to public accommodations and public services, and education. One section of the act, Title VII, specifically bars employers from discriminating against workers on the basis of race, color, religion, or national origin. The legislation applies to most jobs, including professional and management positions.

Women began lobbying Congress to add sex to the list of categories that could not be used by employers to

THIS AMERICAN AIRLINES ADVERTISEMENT OF 1967 ILLUSTRATES THE SEXIST POLICIES PRACTICED AT THE TIME THAT REQUIRED FLIGHT ATTENDANTS TO BE TRIM, YOUNG, AND FEMALE.

discriminate in arriving at hiring and promotion decisions. At first congressmen treated the request as a joke. Supporters of the bill rejected the request because they feared the measure would be defeated if it included protections for women as well as blacks. Women, however, used that perception to their advantage. Members of the National Woman's Party persuaded Representative Howard W. Smith, a Democrat from Virginia, to sponsor an amendment to Title VII that would add sex to the list of protected categories. Smith hoped that the amendment would help defeat the Civil Rights Act, which he opposed.

Congressmen, including Smith, treated the amendment with mocking humor. Emanuel Celler, who supported the Civil Rights Act but opposed the ERA, noted that women were not a minority in his house and did not need protection. "As a matter of fact," the New York Democrat told his colleagues, "the reason I would suggest that we have been living in such harmony . . . is that I usually have the last two words, and those words are, 'Yes, dear.'"

Congressmen roared with laughter. The lone woman on the powerful Ways and Means Committee, Representative Martha Griffiths, rose angrily to address the wisecracking lawmakers. The Congressmen's laughter, she noted, proved the point that women were treated as second-class citizens. In the quiet that followed, Griffiths pointed out that without the amendment, white women would be placed at the bottom of the heap, with little recourse against discrimination. "If you do not add sex to this bill," Griffiths asserted, "you are going to have white men in one bracket, you are going to try to take colored men and colored women and give them equal employment rights, and down at the bottom of the list is going to be a white woman with no rights at all."

Five of the seven female members of Congress spoke for the amendment. Edith Green, a Democrat from

Oregon, criticized the amendment, saying that it would "clutter up" the civil rights bill. Yet several southern Democrats opposed to the Civil Rights Act testified for the amendment and voted for it. Political pundits theorized that the southerners supported the amendment in the hopes that it would kill the overall bill. But others truly favored the amendment, appearing on a Saturday to cast their votes for the additional wording. Many of these supporters were northern Republicans, who also were among the strongest proponents of the ERA. After an afternoon of discussion, the House voted 168 to 133 to add the "sex" wording to Title VII. Two days later, on February 10, 1964, the Civil Rights Act won approval in the House, 289 to 126.

In the Senate, supporters of the civil rights bill threatened to scuttle the sex amendment. President Johnson, a skilled politician, had put together a coalition of Democrats and moderate Republicans to win support for the proposed legislation. The gender debate threw a monkey wrench into the mix. Finally, under pressure from Griffiths, Johnson spoke out in favor of the amendment in April 1964. The National Federation of Business and Professional Women (BPW), with more than 150,000 members throughout the country, lobbied for the bill. When Senate minority leader Everett Dirksen, a key Republican supporter of the Civil Rights Act, said he planned to remove the wording, the BPW rallied support for the cause. Dirksen backed down after women voters in his home state of Illinois mounted a massive campaign— organized by the BPW—and buried him under a barrage of telegrams and letters. A fellow Republican senator, Margaret Chase Smith of Maine, also pressured Dirksen to leave the sex amendment alone.

The swirling debate that ensued focused on civil rights for African Americans. A three month filibuster led by southern Democrats opposed to the act ended when

Dirksen brought in enough Republican votes to shut off the opposition. On June 19, 1964, after the end of the longest debate in Senate history, the Civil Rights Act passed, 73 to 27. President Johnson signed the act on July 2, 1964. It became effective one year later.

Amid the hoopla over civil rights, there was little understanding of the impact the act would have on women's rights. Observers later expressed the view that equal opportunity legislation for women workers never would have passed—at least not for years—had it been introduced on its own. The passage of Title VII was a monumental victory for women that would change the composition of the modern American workplace. Buried in Title VII, that little word "sex" would soon trigger a flood of grievances and lawsuits from women who took the law seriously and were about to force the government to do the same.

A WHOLE NEW BALLGAME

Under the provisions of Title VII, almost all businesses, labor unions, and employers of more than twenty-five workers were barred from discriminating on the basis of race, color, religion, sex, or national origin. They were required by law to evaluate applicants fairly when hiring. The same standards had to be used for all workers eligible for promotions. Workers performing equivalent jobs had to be paid the same wage. No federal statute had ever before required equal treatment from such a broad segment of businesses.

In addition, Title VII established the Equal Employment Opportunity Commission (EEOC), charged it with overseeing the law, and made the new agency responsible for settling disputes between workers and employers. The law gave unsatisfied complainants the right to sue and empowered the attorney general to take action in cases deemed to be "of general public importance."

Among the first to make use of the new law were stewardesses. They had tried and failed to persuade Congress to pass a law protecting older and married women from being laid off as airline hostesses. Immediately tagged "the old broads bill," the legislation was treated as a joke by the nearly all-male Congress. At first the EEOC, being focused on racial discrimination, paid little heed to the stewardesses' complaints. But in November 1966, the commission ruled that the airlines could not legally put age limits on stewardesses without applying the same standard to pilots and other male workers. The EEOC further sided with the stewardesses when it dismissed the airlines' arguments that being single was a prerequisite for the job because married women tended to gain weight and missed more work. Firing women because they married, the EEOC ruled, violated the law.

Another early EEOC case involved the battle to eliminate separate newspaper help-wanted ads for men and women. Initially the EEOC declined to rule against the gender-specific ads. EEOC acting chair Luther Holcomb wrote in the summer of 1966, "Column headings do not prevent persons of either sex from scanning the area of the jobs-available page." An irate Martha Griffiths responded, "I have never entered a door labeled 'Men,' and I doubt that Mr. Holcomb has frequently entered the women's room."

The EEOC's attitude enraged many others as well. Frustrated over the commission's inaction, member Aileen Hernandez resigned and joined feminist author Betty Friedan and others to form a new national organization devoted to women's rights. The National Organization for Women soon attracted hundreds, then thousands, of women and men. After spearheading nationwide protests and filing suit against the EEOC, NOW successfully persuaded the commission to revise its guidelines to ban gender-specific ads.

"PUT YOUR MONEY DOWN AND SIGN YOUR NAME"

The Civil Rights Act of 1964 promised hope for women who wanted their share of the American pie. Title VII of the act included a ban on sex discrimination on the job. The effectiveness of the legislation, however, lay in its enforcement. The Equal Employment Opportunity Commission (EEOC), formed to enforce the act, took a less-than-aggressive stance on sex discrimination in the workplace. The commission voted 3 to 2 to allow employers to advertise for male or female workers and to specify whether jobs were for men or women only. Allowing such ads effectively barred women from higher-paying jobs traditionally held by men.

This infuriated Betty Friedan, author of *The Feminine Mystique*, the groundbreaking book on women's roles. She and others who shared her views met in June 1966 to discuss the possibility of forming an organization that could promote women's rights in the same way civil rights groups had fought for equality for African Americans. At the luncheon meeting, Catherine Conroy, a telephone operator who was a member of Wisconsin's commission for women, pulled out a dollar bill and challenged the others to "put your money down and sign your name." The group adopted the initials NOW that Friedan had scrawled on a napkin.

From that first informal gathering, the National Organization for Women was born. By October 1966, some three hundred men and women had signed up as charter members of the organization. At NOW's first conference on October 29 to 30, 1966, in Washington, D.C., members adopted a statement of purpose that pledged "to take action to bring women into full participation in the mainstream of American society now, exercising all the privileges and responsibilities thereof in truly equal partnership with men." In the statement, the members noted that the time had come "for a new movement toward true equality for all women in America . . . as part of the world-wide revolution of human rights now taking place within and beyond our national borders."

Members elected Friedan as president and Aileen Hernandez as executive vice president. Richard Graham served as the first vice president, and Caroline Davis as secretary-treasurer. Kay Clarenbach was elected to chair the board. Hernandez, as a member of the EEOC, had always voted against sex-segregated help-wanted ads. One of the group's first actions aimed at banning the ads' designation of jobs as "male" and "female."

The group eventually attracted thousands of supporters, male and female, who worked tirelessly in the failed effort to ratify the equal rights amendment. Beginning in 1968 NOW members began picketing facilities that barred women and demanded that they be given equal access to all public accommodations. In other actions, the group pushed for equal opportunities for women in business, education, sports, and the military. Members led efforts to improve child care services and to help victims of rape and other violence. NOW also participated in many court cases, including *Roberts* v. *U.S. Jaycees*, in support of women's rights.

In 2006 NOW and its more than 500,000 members celebrated the organization's forty-year campaign to win equal treatment for women. As the nation's leading women's rights group, NOW continues to focus on issues that affect women and that threaten their right to equal treatment under the law.

BETTY FRIEDAN, AUTHOR OF THE GROUNDBREAKING BOOK *THE FEMININE MYSTIQUE*, POSES AT HER DESK IN NEW YORK IN 1970. THE WRITER WAS ONE OF THE FOUNDERS OF THE NATIONAL ORGANIZATION FOR WOMEN.

Despite the new rules, several newspapers continued to run ads under Help Wanted–Male and Help Wanted–Female headings. NOW filed a complaint against the *Pittsburgh Press* in October 1969 to force the newspaper to discontinue the practice. In 1973, in *Pittsburgh Press Company* v. *Pittsburgh Commission on Human Relations*, the U.S. Supreme Court ruled against the newspaper. The 5 to 4 decision, delivered by Justice Lewis Powell, concluded that use of male/female headings in want ads violated the antidiscrimination provisions of Title VII. "By implication at least," Powell wrote, "an advertiser whose want ad appears in the 'Jobs–Male Interest' column is likely to discriminate against women in his hiring decisions." The Court attached to the decision a sampling of male and female want ads published on January 4, 1970. Annual salaries for the "men's" jobs ranged from $7,200 to $30,000, while the "women's" positions offered far less, from $4,200 to $13,000.

In 1972 Congress passed another piece of landmark legislation to strengthen the powers of the EEOC. The Equal Employment Opportunity Act of 1972 aimed "to further promote equal employment opportunities for American workers." The act authorized the EEOC to sue violators of Title VII. It also expanded the ban on discriminatory employment practices to cover educational institutions; state, federal, and local government employers; and businesses with fifteen (instead of twenty-five) or more employees. Those filing complaints under Title VII were given up to 300 days to submit their claims, and a longer time (90 days) to file suit after EEOC issued findings on a case.

OTHER COURT RULINGS

Several other Supreme Court rulings expanded working women's rights. The 1971 case of *Phillips* v. *Martin Marietta Corp.* marked the first Title VII grievance to be presented to the Supreme Court. The petitioner, Ida Phillips, was a Florida mother whose application for a job at Martin Marietta had been rejected because she had young children. The company hired men with preschool-age children but not women. In a unanimous decision, the Court decreed that the company's policy illegally discriminated against women under the provisions of Title VII.

The case was one of many that would unite advocates for

civil rights for African Americans, women, union members, and other groups. Two of the lawyers arguing for Phillips, Jack Greenberg and James M. Nabrit III, had played prominent roles in several Supreme Court cases involving the rights of African Americans, including *Brown* v. *Board of Education*, the landmark suit that resulted in the banning of segregation in the public schools. Among those filing briefs supporting Phillips's cause were the American Civil Liberties Union (ACLU), NOW, the Air Line Stewards and Stewardesses Association (a branch of the AFL-CIO), and the Human Rights for Women organization.

In another 1971 case, *Reed* v. *Reed*, the Court linked women's rights to the guarantees provided in the Fourteenth Amendment's equal protection clause. The petitioner, Sally Reed, challenged an Idaho law that gave preference to men in naming administrators of the estates of people who had died without leaving a will. The Court unanimously agreed that the law illegally discriminated against women. Chief Justice Warren Burger, who delivered the decision, wrote, "To give a mandatory preference to members of either sex over members of the other, merely to accomplish the elimination of hearings on the merits, is to make the very kind of arbitrary legislative choice forbidden by the Equal Protection Clause of the Fourteenth Amendment."

Women gained access to equal military benefits as the result of a 1973 Supreme Court ruling in *Frontiero* v. *Richardson*. The 8 to 1 decision, which extended equal rights protections to women in the military, gave female officers in the U.S. Air Force the same housing and medical benefits provided to male officers. Ruth Bader Ginsburg, who would later be appointed to the Supreme Court, argued the case for the petitioner Sharron Frontiero.

Other decisions followed that awarded women equal

Social Security benefits and made it illegal for employers to exclude women applicants from jobs on the basis of minimum height and weight requirements unrelated to the work. A 1975 case, *Taylor* v. *Louisiana*, required women as well as men to serve on juries. Until then, only women who volunteered for jury duty served as jurors. The Supreme Court also barred school boards from firing teachers simply because they were pregnant.

Not all the Court decisions favored women. The ruling in a 1979 case, *Personnel Administrator of Massachusetts* v. *Feeney*, allowed government employers to give veterans— almost all of whom were male—preferential treatment in hiring. Since women were barred from many military jobs, the ruling dramatically reduced job opportunities for women in certain areas of government. In its 7 to 2 decision, the Supreme Court concluded that the law did not specifically discriminate against women, since male nonveterans also were at a disadvantage and women who were veterans could benefit from the policy. Favoring veterans, the Court decided, served "legitimate and worthy purposes" and had not been enacted as a means to discriminate against women.

WILLIAM L. WILSON, COMMISSIONER OF THE MINNESOTA DEPARTMENT OF HUMAN RIGHTS IN 1979, FOUND PROBABLE CAUSE THAT THE JAYCEES HAD VIOLATED THE STATE'S ANTIDISCRIMINATION LAW.

FIVE
MINNESOTA TAKES ON THE CASE

THE CAMPAIGN TO PASS the equal rights amendment, though ultimately unsuccessful, demonstrated that the majority of states supported equal rights for women. Decisions by the Supreme Court and by the lower courts reinforced the legitimacy of women's rights. During the 1970s and 1980s many states adopted their own version of the ERA or put in place laws and policies to combat discrimination based on sex.

Long before the Minnesota group filed its complaint against the national Jaycees in December 1978, the state had adopted several laws to protect women from discrimination. In 1969 Minnesota added a provision to its state Act Against Discrimination making it illegal for employers to "unreasonably exclude" applicants based on their sex. The 1973 state legislature extended protections against sexual discrimination to apply to housing, public accommodations, public service, credit, and education. The new law also barred employers, landlords, and others from discriminating against people because of their marital status. The law incorporated language originally adopted in 1955 that such discrimination "threatens the rights and privileges of the inhabitants of this state and menaces the institutions and foundations of democracy." Additional regulations passed in 1977 protected pregnant women against discrimination on the job.

Several similar cases had already made their way to court in other states. Local chapters of NOW and groups of parents had sued Little League Baseball Inc. to open up the sports organization to girls. By 1974, fifty-seven suits had been filed against the Little League in more than a dozen states. In one case the New Jersey Superior Court ruled that the state's public accommodations law prohibited Little League Baseball from excluding girls. In response, the national baseball club allowed girls on its teams in 1974.

STATE HEARING

As in the New Jersey case, the Jaycees' case focused on public accommodations law. On January 25, 1979, Minnesota Department of Human Rights commissioner William L. Wilson found probable cause that the Jaycees had violated the state's antidiscrimination law that gave women full access to public accommodations. He put the case on the calendar of the state hearing examiner. Determined to block the state hearing, the national Jaycees filed suit in U.S. District Court. The organization claimed that the state's action violated its members' First Amendment rights of freedom to associate with whomever they chose.

The court allowed the hearing to proceed. On April 23, 1979, people representing the state, the local Jaycees, and the national organization gathered in a fifth-floor office of the Metro Square Building in St. Paul to tell their side of the story. For two days, hearing examiner George Beck listened to testimony in the matter. Richard L. Varco Jr., a St. Paul attorney, oversaw the case for the state and the local chapters. Carl D. Hall Jr. of Tulsa, Oklahoma, and Clay R. Moore of Minneapolis represented the national Jaycees.

Eight witnesses testified at the St. Paul hearing. The state presented ninety-nine written exhibits, including

CARL D. HALL JR., THE JAYCEES' ATTORNEY, ANSWERS REPORTERS' QUESTIONS AFTER ARGUING HIS CASE BEFORE THE SUPREME COURT ON APRIL 18, 1984.

statements by male and female members of local Jaycees chapters that the national Jaycees discriminated against women. Among the ten exhibits on display by the national Jaycees were the bylaws and roster of Kiwanis International, another national all-men's group. The Jaycees argued that forcing its chapters to admit women would destroy the purpose of the organization and interfere with First Amendment rights of its members.

During the hearing, Kathryn Ebert, Kathleen Hawn, and Sally Pedersen told how membership in the Jaycees had benefited their careers. Male Jaycees from Minnesota also testified, sharing their views on why women should be admitted to the organization as full members.

While the controversy over women members simmered, many members left the St. Paul chapter and formed their own organization. Along with the former president of the local Jaycees club, 250 men and 93 women joined the St. Paul Community Business Leaders group. The new club welcomed men and women alike, but otherwise had the same goals and programs as the Jaycees. Fewer than two dozen men remained in the Jaycees' St. Paul chapter.

On October 9, 1979, examiner Beck issued his ruling. The national Jaycees, he said, had "committed an unfair discriminatory practice" in violation of Minnesota law. "It would make little sense to guarantee women an equal opportunity in employment while denying them access to activities designed to help in career advancement," the ruling noted. Beck ordered the national Jaycees to reinstate the charters of the state chapters and barred the group from denying membership to anyone in Minnesota on the basis of sex.

Jaycees sue

Three weeks after Beck issued his directive, the national Jaycees sued the state of Minnesota in U.S. District Court. The Jaycees' suit named Marilyn McClure, who had taken Wilson's place as human rights commissioner, so the case was called *U.S. Jaycees* v. *McClure*.

Shortly after the Jaycees filed suit, the Michigan legislature expanded the state's antidiscrimination laws. In 1980 it made illegal any practice that would "deny any person the full and equal enjoyment of the services, privileges and advantages of a place of public accommodation because of sex."

The Jaycees, in court documents, claimed to be a private club and asserted that the state had no jurisdiction over its policies on membership. The group's lawyers continued to argue that the state's ruling violated its members' right to associate with men only. The First Amendment, they contended, guarantees citizens the freedom to meet with people of their own choosing and, moreover, the state could not force members of a private voluntary association to include women in their gatherings.

For its part, the state argued that the Jaycees was a public accommodation because it sold memberships, training manuals, courses, and goods such as T-shirts and other items to the public. All public accommodations, the state contended, had to abide by antidiscrimination laws.

Before proceeding with the case, the district court asked the Minnesota Supreme Court to define the meaning of public accommodation as the term was used in the state's human rights act. In response, the state's high court ruled that the Jaycees was indeed a public accommodation. The club qualified as a business, the court ruled, because it sold goods and services to a large segment of the public and treated its members more like customers than owners. Furthermore, the Jaycees was a public, rather than a private, club because it did not confine its members to a small, elite group. Members did not have to pass tests, hold particular political views, or meet other qualifying factors. In fact, all could join as long as they paid their dues and were males between the ages of eighteen and thirty-five.

With that ruling in hand, the district court tried the case in August 1981. The decision, delivered March 15, 1982, favored the state and the local chapters. The court ordered the Jaycees to accept women as full members. "Young men have the right to associate with whomever they please," the ruling stated, "but under Minnesota law they should not be able to form an organization that is primarily business oriented and exclude young women from that organization when the effect of that exclusion is to deprive the latter of an equal opportunity for leadership positions."

Within a month, the Jaycees had filed a notice of appeal with the U.S. Court of Appeals for the Eighth Circuit. The club's lawyers based the appeal on three points:

- The Jaycees operated as a private club.
- The Minnesota Supreme Court's definition of public

accommodations was unconstitutionally vague.
• The ruling by the lower court infringed on members'
right to free speech and association.

TOUGH STAND AGAINST DISCRIMINATION

As the suit made its way through the court system, Minnesota continued to beef up its antidiscrimination laws.
The state's Human Rights Act of 1982 expanded the ban on
discrimination in public places and defined public accommodations as "a business, accommodation, refreshment,
entertainment, recreation, or transportation facility of
any kind, whether licensed or not, whose goods, services,
facilities, privileges, advantages or accommodations are
extended, offered, sold, or otherwise made available to the
public." Under the new act, it became illegal "to deny any
person the full and equal enjoyment of the goods, services,
facilities, privileges, advantages, and accommodations of a
place of public accommodation because of race, color,
creed, religion, disability, national origin or sex."

In a 1983 case similar to that of the Jaycees, the New
York State Court of Appeals (the state's highest court)
ruled that the U.S. Power Squadrons operating in New
York could not exclude women from membership. The
Power Squadrons, a private group of boating enthusiasts
with national headquarters in Raleigh, North Carolina,
allowed women to participate in water safety classes but
barred them as full members. In making its ruling, the
court tightened the definition of public accommodation
beyond just a physical location. The term, according to the
court, also included "the idea . . . in the broad sense of
providing conveniences and services to the public." The
court further ruled that people could not circumvent the
law merely by forming private clubs with the purpose of
excluding a particular group of people (usually, at that
time, blacks or women). "Though nominally private," the

court decreed, "[clubs] are not exempt from the provisions of the Human Rights Law if they are not in fact private except for purposes of discrimination."

A Reversal

At the court hearing that followed, the state repeated its assertions that for the Jaycees to bar women members was a violation of state law. This time, though, the court sided with the Jaycees. On June 7, 1983, two of the three appeals court judges voted to overturn the district court ruling, rejecting the state supreme court's definition as too vague to be valid. The appeals panel agreed with the Jaycees that the state action had interfered with members' First Amendment rights. It suggested the state could encourage the Jaycees to change its membership policies by subtler methods, perhaps by eliminating the club's tax benefits or barring state officials from being members of the club.

The lone member of the panel to support the state's claims, Judge Donald P. Lay, issued a stinging dissent. Lay wrote that the Jaycees' membership policies were based on an antiquated system that "relegated women to a status inferior to that of men."

The reversal stunned state officials and local Jaycees members. Several U.S. Supreme Court cases had invalidated claims by restaurants, schools, and other groups that their status as private clubs allowed them to circumvent the law by excluding African Americans. Several U.S. Supreme Court cases had overruled the strategy. Now the same ruse was being used to block women's participation, and the court, at least one federal appeals court, had allowed it.

Advocates for women's rights, including Minnesota state officials, vowed not to accept defeat. They would take the case to the Supreme Court. On October 31, 1983, attorneys for the state of Minnesota submitted a request that the nation's highest court hear their appeal.

Members of the U.S. Supreme Court in 1982, front row, from left: Justices Thurgood Marshall and William Brennan Jr., Chief Justice Warren Burger, Justices Byron White and Harry Blackmun. Back row, from left: Justices John Paul Stevens, Lewis Powell Jr., William Rehnquist, and Sandra Day O'Connor

SIX
MAKING THE CASE

EVERY year THOUSANDS of people, businesses, organizations, and government entities apply to the U.S. Supreme Court for a hearing. As the highest judicial body in the land, the Supreme Court is the last hope for those who have lost their appeals in lower courts. The Court's decisions are final.

The Supreme Court term usually runs from October through June. To win a spot on the busy docket, appellants usually file a petition for certiorari (meaning "to be informed of"). This document, a formal request for a hearing, briefly outlines the issues involved, lists the parties, and gives reasons for asking the Court to hear the case. The justices decide in private conferences which of the numerous cases presented they will review.

On January 9, 1984, the Supreme Court announced it would hear arguments in the Jaycees case. The Court docket listed the case as *Gomez-Bethke* v. *U.S. Jaycees*. At the time, Irene Gomez-Bethke served as Minnesota's human rights commissioner, having replaced Marilyn McClure. By the time the case was decided, on July 3, 1984, Kathryn R. Roberts was acting commissioner, and the case ultimately was listed as *Roberts* v. *U.S. Jaycees*. Oral arguments were scheduled to be held before the Court on April 18, 1984.

NOT SO Brief Arguments

Before arguing at a formal Supreme Court hearing, lawyers on both sides must present their case in legal documents called briefs. Despite the name, briefs filed with the Court fill many pages. Lawyers discuss the issues involved at length, detail the history of the case, and make arguments based on laws and previous rulings delivered by the Supreme Court and the lower courts. A brief can take months to research and prepare. Supreme Court justices read these detailed summaries carefully before deciding how to vote. In some cases, a justice will borrow ideas from a well-prepared brief in writing his or her opinion.

Richard L. Varco Jr., hired as special assistant attorney general to represent Minnesota's position in the case, prepared the state's brief. He received help from the attorney general's office and Kent G. Harbison, chief deputy attorney general. He packed the state's arguments into thirty-four pages and cited several cases that involved racial discrimination. The brief was filed on February 23, 1984.

Carl D. Hall Jr. and Clay R. Moore, the lawyers who had handled the Jaycees' case in the past, composed the club's arguments. In their fifty-page brief, the lawyers focused on members' First Amendment rights and the vagueness of the Minnesota public accommodations law. They filed the brief with the Court a month later, on March 22.

Many cases that come before the U.S. Supreme Court address issues that are of importance to groups beyond those directly involved in the matter. Often these groups file their own briefs to make points for the petitioner (the side appealing the lower court's judgment) or for the respondent (the side that won in lower court). The Latin term for such groups is *amicus curiae*, or friend of the court. In the *Roberts* case, groups lined up to add their arguments to the court record. Seven entities filed briefs

RICHARD L. VARCO JR. REPRESENTED THE STATE OF MINNESOTA IN THE *ROBERTS* CASE.

supporting the state and the local chapters. National organizations included the ACLU, which for decades had championed the civil rights of African Americans and members of other unfairly treated groups; the Legal Defense and Education Fund of the National Association for the Advancement of Colored People (NAACP), a leader in pushing for African Americans' rights in court; the National League of Cities; and the Women's Issues Network. In addition, the St. Paul Community Business Leaders, founded by former members of the St. Paul Jaycees; the Alliance for Women Membership; and the states of New York and California all filed amicus briefs supporting Minnesota's position. A multistate firm,

THrouGH THe courT sYsTem

First Stop: State Court Cases
Almost all cases (about 95 percent) start in state courts. These courts go by various names, depending on the state in which they operate, such as circuit, district, municipal, county, or superior. The case is tried and decided by a judge, a panel of judges, or a jury.
The side that loses can then appeal to the next level.

First Stop: Federal Court Cases
U.S. DISTRICT COURT—About 5 percent of cases begin their journey in a federal court. Most of these cases concern federal laws, the U.S. Constitution, or disputes that involve two or more states. They are heard in one of the ninety-four U.S. district courts in the nation.
U.S. COURT OF INTERNATIONAL TRADE—Federal court cases involving international trade appear in the U.S. Court of International Trade.
U.S. COURT OF FEDERAL CLAIMS—The U.S. Court of Federal Claims hears federal cases against the U.S. government that involve more than $10,000, Indian tribes, and some disputes with government contractors. The loser in federal court can appeal to the next level.

Appeals: State Cases
Forty states have appeals courts that hear cases from the state courts. Cases from states without an appeals court go directly to the state supreme court.

Appeals: Federal Cases
U.S. FEDERAL APPEALS COURTS—There are thirteen federal appellate courts: twelve U.S. circuit courts that handle cases appealed from the U.S. district courts and one U.S. Court of Appeals that decides cases appealed

from the U.S. Court of International Trade and the U.S. Court of Federal Claims.

Each district court and every state and territory are assigned to one of the twelve circuits. Appeals in a few state cases—those that deal with rights guaranteed by the U.S. Constitution—are also heard in the circuit courts. Among the cases heard in the U.S. Court of Appeals are those involving patents and minor claims against the federal government.

Further Appeals: State Supreme Court

Cases appealed from state appeals courts go to the highest courts in the state—usually called the supreme court. In New York, however, the state's highest court is called the court of appeals. Few state cases go beyond this point.

Final Appeals: U.S. Supreme Court

The U.S. Supreme Court is the highest court in the country. Its decision on a case is the final word. The Court rules on issues that can affect every person in the nation. It has decided cases on slavery, abortion, school segregation, and many other important issues.

The Court selects the cases it will hear—around seventy-five each year. Four of the nine justices must vote to consider a case in order for it to be heard. Almost all cases have been appealed from the lower courts (either state or federal).

Most people seeking a decision from the Court submit a petition for *certiorari*, outlining the case and giving reasons why the Court should review it. If the petition is accepted—that is if certiorari is granted—the case will be moved from a lower court to the high court for review. The Court receives more than nine thousand of these requests annually.

On rare occasions, when an issue must be decided

immediately, the Court will allow a case of national importance to bypass the lower court. In 1971, for example, the Court agreed to hear directly the so-called Pentagon Papers case, *New York Times* v. *United States*. To win a spot on the Court's docket, a case must fall within one of the following categories:

- Disputes between states and the federal government or between two or more states.

- Cases involving ambassadors, consuls, and foreign ministers.

- Appeals from state courts that have ruled on a federal question.

- Appeals from federal appeals courts in cases in which appellate courts have issued conflicting decisions (about two-thirds of all requests fall into this category).

Northwestern Bell Telephone Company, submitted a request to file a brief on behalf of the state and the women members.

Two all-male organizations—Rotary International and the Boy Scouts of America—and an association representing private clubs—the Conference of Private Organizations—filed briefs supporting the Jaycees' ban on membership for women. The first two groups would face their own court challenges to membership.

Minnesota's case
In the state's brief, Varco argued that the appeals court had made three errors in deciding for the Jaycees. First, he said, the First Amendment does not automatically guarantee people the right to associate with anyone they please under all circumstances. Although the First Amendment specifically guarantees the right to assemble, or gather together in a group, it makes no mention of freedom of association, which would give people the right to choose the group's members. Varco argued that the freedom of association is protected by the Constitution only when a specified freedom, such as speech or religion, is also threatened. He backed up this point by citing several Supreme Court cases that limited a group's right to exclude people. In a 1945 case, *Railway Mail Ass'n v. Corsi*, the Court ruled that New York labor unions could not exclude people because of race, color, or creed. In a more recent case, decided in 1976, the court overruled a group who wanted to keep black students out of the private school their children attended.

Varco used another case, *NAACP v. Alabama ex rel. Patterson*, decided in 1958, to illustrate a situation in which the right to associate was essential to preserving a group's free speech. In that case, Alabama officials had tried to force the state branch of the NAACP to report the names and addresses of its members. The Court allowed the group to keep the information secret because revealing it would likely have subjected the members to harassment, threats, and hostility when the NAACP took an unpopular stand.

The Jaycees, however, faced no such threats to its free speech if women were admitted as members, Varco concluded. The organization could continue to take public stands on issues and pursue the same goals. The lawyer drove home the point:

> Allowing women to vote, hold office, and receive awards will therefore change nothing about the organization except its sexually restrictive nature. . . . The Jaycees can point to no organizational goal to which women cannot and do not aspire, no organizational function which women cannot perform, and no organizational position regarding which sex mandates a point of view.

Varco then addressed the appeals court's second error: the state's goal of preventing sex discrimination was more compelling than the Jaycees' desire to maintain an all-male membership. He equated the suggestion that women could take other avenues to improve their careers to the old "separate but equal" argument posed by segregationists in the South in the years before the *Brown* decision, If the Supreme Court allowed that reasoning to stand, Varco argued, then business owners could keep certain groups of people out of their shops as long as there were other stores they could patronize.

The lawyer's third point focused on the Minnesota Supreme Court's definition of public accommodation. Disagreeing with the appeals court's ruling that the definition was unconstitutionally vague, Varco described the wording as "clear and unambiguous." He concluded with a plea that the Court reverse the decision and order the Jaycees to allow women to join the club.

Jaycees' Brief

The lawyers presenting the Jaycees' case centered on three main points: the members' right of association, the vagueness of the Minnesota law, and the law's "chilling impact" on private clubs. Allowing women to join the group as full members, the brief argued, would "effectively destroy the Jaycees' ability to achieve its core purpose, namely, furthering the interest of young men. The Jaycees would no longer be able to confine the central reason for its existence to the advancement of the interest of young men, but must also serve the interests of young women."

Women members, the lawyers contended, would have views on issues that differed from those held by men. Their votes would alter the focus of the group, and in doing so, would change the public stands an all-male association would take. That, the Jaycees argued, infringed on the group's freedom of speech.

Hall and Moore disputed the state's designation of the Jaycees as a public accommodation. The organization was a private club whose members owned and directed the operation, they wrote, not a public restaurant or other business. The lawyers noted that other groups, such as Kiwanis and Rotary, had similar policies that excluded women. The Minnesota law gave no guidance on how to distinguish between clubs that could and could not exclude women, and the state supreme court's definition provided no answer. Therefore, the lawyers contended, Minnesota's law on public accommodations was too vague and should be ruled unconstitutional.

In addition, Hall and Moore argued that the law was too broad and would affect all private organizations. Under the law, they said, women's groups could be required to accept men, and religious groups would have to open their doors to people of other faiths. The freedom of Americans to form private clubs "created a culturally rich and pluralistic society," the lawyers told the Court. To eliminate that freedom by reversing the appeals court ruling, they argued, would destroy "the right of the people to decide for themselves who shall be their friends and associational companions."

Shortly after the Jaycees filed its brief, the state delivered a short rebuttal. That the Jaycees had formed to serve a particular group (young men) did not give the club immunity from state law, Varco contended. He also dismissed the Jaycees' claim that female members would prevent male members from speaking freely or from benefiting from the advantages offered by the club. Women, like men, Varco pointed out, hold a variety of opinions. "One's position on the issues," he wrote, "is not determined by one's sex."

AMICUS BRIEFS

Northwestern Bell Telephone Company's statement to the Court addressed the issue from the viewpoint of a major employer. Supporting the state's side, the telephone company argued that it was injured by the Jaycees' policies that prevented female Bell workers from participating in the full range of opportunities presented by the club. The company noted that it had benefited in particular from a female employee's stint as president of the Minneapolis chapter in 1981 and 1982. The national group's resistance to women members, the memorandum continued, undercut efforts by the company and by the state to attain equal treatment for men and women in the workplace. It concluded: "For so long as the U.S. Jaycees, an esteemed business organization, discriminates against women in its

FORMER MEMBERS OF A BOY SCOUT TROOP GIVE THE SCOUT SALUTE. THE ORGANIZATION FILED A BRIEF IN SUPPORT OF THE JAYCEES' RIGHT TO EXCLUDE WOMEN FROM MEMBERSHIP. THE BOY SCOUTS LATER WON ITS CASE IN THE SUPREME COURT TO EXCLUDE GAY MEN FROM LEADERSHIP POSITIONS. LOWER COURTS HAVE RULED THAT THE GROUP CAN CONTINUE TO BAR GIRLS FROM MEMBERSHIP IN THE SCOUTS.

ranks, equal opportunity for positions of leadership and advancement in employment will not be achieved."

The National Organization for Women, a major force in the push to ratify the ERA, contended in its brief that the Jaycees provided "members with an entree to the 'Old Boys' Network'" and that women's careers suffered when they were excluded from membership.

The Boy Scouts of America, who like the Jaycees had a

male-only membership, took an opposite stand. In its brief, the organization argued that the state's interest in opening the Jaycees' membership to women was not compelling enough to justify overriding the constitutional rights of the male members. According to the brief, the state should interfere with private clubs only to ensure public health or safety or other "compelling" reason.

After reviewing the briefs, the justices would hear the lawyers on each side of the case argue the merits of their positions. The lawyers would have less than a month to prepare for oral arguments, scheduled to take place at the Supreme Court's Washington, D.C., courtroom on April 18, 1984.

seven
BEFORE THE COURT

A LAWYER ARGUING before the U.S. Supreme Court approaches the bench with a mixture of exhilaration and dread. Nine black-robed justices peer down from their raised leather seats as the speaker struggles to sound both profound and sincere. The austere grandness of the courtroom, with its massive oak door, marble columns, and red velvet drapes, gives a sense of the history that has transpired within its walls.

Even the most accomplished lawyers quake at the daunting task of presenting a strong, clear argument while taking care not to cross swords with nine very distinct personalities. Justices can interrupt at any time to ask questions or make comments, a practice that has thrown more than one nervous lawyer off track. Presenting oral arguments before the Supreme Court can also be an attorney's most exciting experience—and one that brings great prestige. Ruth Bader Ginsburg, who later joined the "brethren" as the Court's second female justice, has recalled her anxiety during oral arguments in the 1973 *Frontiero* case, followed by a "feeling of extraordinary power." She won the case, despite the C+ rating Justice Harry A. Blackmun had awarded her in his private notes.

William Wirt, a U.S. attorney general of the early 1800s who argued more than a hundred cases before the Court, knew the difficulty of pleasing the justices. He advised lawyers facing the assignment to "read like [Thomas] Jefferson and speak like [Patrick] Henry. . . . Master the cause in all of its points of fact and law; digest a profound, comprehensive, simple, and glowing speech for the occasion. . . . And insinuate yourself among the heartstrings, the bones, and the marrow."

No doubt anxiety dogged the lawyers in the *Jaycees* case as they climbed up the marble steps of the Supreme Court building the morning of April 18, 1984. The sky was overcast but the weather was mild, a typical spring day in the nation's capital. Richard L. Varco Jr. and Carl D. Hall Jr. entered the chamber and waited in leather chairs facing the bench. All rose as the nine justices filed in from behind the velvet drapes. Chief Justice Warren Burger led the way, followed by the associate justices, whose order of entrance was, as always, determined by their length of service on the Court.

THE JUSTICES

The chief justice had served as both assistant attorney general and appeals court judge before joining the Court in 1969. He and Associate Justice Blackmun had been childhood friends in Minnesota, and both had been named to the bench by President Richard M. Nixon. Neither justice would vote on the *Jaycees* case. Chief Justice Burger had served as president of the St. Paul Jaycees in 1935, and Blackmun had been a member of the Minneapolis chapter. Both, however, appeared in Court and participated in the questioning of the lawyers presenting the case.

Justice William J. Brennan Jr., appointed in 1956, led the liberal wing of the Court. Nominated by President Dwight D. Eisenhower, he had been on the bench longer than any of his fellow justices. Brennan had served on the New Jersey Superior Court and as an associate judge

CHIEF JUSTICE WARREN BURGER HEADED THE SUPREME COURT DURING THE TIME THE *ROBERTS* V. *JAYCEES* CASE WAS DECIDED, BUT HE AND JUSTICE HARRY BLACKMUN DID NOT VOTE ON THE MATTER BECAUSE BOTH HAD BEEN MEMBERS OF THE MINNEAPOLIS JAYCEES.

on that state's supreme court before being named to the high court.

Justice Byron R. White, one of only two justices nominated by President John F. Kennedy, had served as deputy U.S. attorney general in Kennedy's administration. Although White had voted against the majority in the controversial 1973 abortion rights case *Roe* v. *Wade*, White had taken other stands favoring women's equality since his appointment in 1962.

Justice Thurgood Marshall, the Court's only African-American member, was nominated to his post by President Lyndon B. Johnson in 1967. As lead attorney for the NAACP in the cases that led to the 1954 ruling in *Brown* v. *Board of Education*, Marshall had played a prominent role in the battle to desegregate the nation's schools. Marshall usually sided with the liberal wing of the Court.

Justices Lewis F. Powell Jr. and William H. Rehnquist, Nixon appointees, took their oaths of office in 1972. Rehnquist, who, like White, had voted against the majority in *Roe* v. *Wade*, was considered to be the Court's most conservative member. In several previous cases involving women's rights, he had voted against the majority and asserted a woman's role as wife and mother. Powell, a prominent corporate lawyer before his service on the bench, became known as the Court's centrist, a moderate who helped balance the liberal and conservative wings.

Justice John Paul Stevens joined the Court in 1975, having been nominated by President Gerald R. Ford. A moderate Republican, Stevens had been an antitrust lawyer, a law professor, and an appeals court judge. Known as an independent thinker, he cast votes with both the conservative and liberal blocs.

Justice Sandra Day O'Connor, the newest member of the Court and the only woman, had been on the Court less than three years when the *Jaycees* case was argued.

Nominated by President Ronald Reagan in 1981, she initially was identified as a conservative but later occupied a centrist position on the Court. As one of relatively few women to enter the legal profession in the 1950s, she had had difficulty finding a job after graduating third in her class from Stanford Law School. She eventually started her own law firm and went on to become a judge on the Arizona Court of Appeals.

THE STATE'S ARGUMENT

At 11:37 a.m. Chief Justice Burger signaled to Varco to begin his argument. The lawyer focused his opening remarks on the Jaycees organization. He noted that the club had a vast nationwide network of seven thousand chapters throughout the United States. In 1980, the lawyer said, the Jaycees had 295,000 members, 40 employees, a $2 million budget, extensive training programs, and aggressive recruiting and marketing campaigns. "What [this] shows," he told the Court, "is that [the Jaycees club] operates the way a business operates. Businesses go out and seek customers. They go out on a continuous basis to look for people to buy their products."

Justice Rehnquist compared the Jaycees' recruitment of new members to that of college fraternities, but Varco noted that the Jaycees were not as selective as a private social club might be in seeking people to join the group. He acknowledged that, like a fraternity, the Jaycees accepted only young people. Its bylaws stipulated that members be between the ages of eighteen and thirty-five. Such a requirement discriminated against older people, Varco acknowledged, but added that Minnesota had no law against age discrimination. The Jaycees' recruitment techniques were relevant to the case, Varco said, because they showed that the club acted as a business, rather than as a private club, which might not be bound by the

Justice Sandra Day O'Connor

Sandra Day O'Connor could drive a truck, fire a rifle, and ride a pony by the time she was eight. She had a bobcat for a pet, and her best friends were cowboys.

Intelligent and practical, O'Connor overcame discrimination against women, found her way around roadblocks, and in 1981 became the first woman to serve on the U.S. Supreme Court. Opening the door to what had always been a men-only preserve, the fifty-one-year-old jurist overcame one more barrier to women in her profession. It was a role she had played many times.

Born in Texas in 1930, O'Connor spent most of her childhood on her family's ranch in Arizona, where she developed an independent, practical outlook on life. During the school year, she lived with her grandmother in El Paso, Texas, where she attended a private girls' school. In 1950, at age twenty, she graduated magna cum laude from Stanford University, where she had studied economics. When her family's ranch became embroiled in a legal dispute, she became interested in the law. Two years later she had earned a law degree from Stanford Law School. Classmate William H. Rehnquist (later chief justice of the United States) earned the top spot among the graduates.

Although O'Connor had placed third in a class of 102, the new lawyer could not find a job. Established law firms refused to hire a woman. Only one prestigious firm offered her work, not as a lawyer but as a legal secretary. One of the firm's partners, William French Smith, would later serve as U.S. attorney general. In that position, he would urge President Ronald Reagan to consider O'Connor to fill the Supreme Court seat vacated by Potter Stewart.

Back in the early 1950s, O'Connor had rejected the

Justice Sandra Day O'Connor, the first woman to serve on the U.S. Supreme Court, voted with the majority in requiring the Jaycees to admit women members.

offer for secretarial work and became deputy county attorney in San Mateo, California. She later accompanied her husband, John O'Connor, to Germany, where she served as a civilian lawyer for three years. John O'Connor, also a lawyer, was another graduate of Stanford Law, where the two had met.

After the couple returned to Arizona, O'Connor again had trouble finding a job and in 1958 set up her own law firm with a partner. In 1960 she took time off to raise three sons, then rejoined the workforce as an assistant state attorney in Arizona in 1965. The governor appointed her to fill a vacancy in the state senate four years later. An active volunteer for the Republican party, O'Connor went on to win reelection and later became the first woman in the nation to serve as majority leader in a state senate.

In 1974 she won election as a judge on the Maricopa County Superior Court. Five years later she was appointed to the Arizona Court of Appeals. President Reagan nominated her to the U.S. Supreme Court on August 19, 1981, and the Senate confirmed her in a unanimous vote on September 25. When O'Connor took her seat on the bench, her fellow justices ended the two-hundred-year-old tradition of referring to one another as "Mr. Justice" and switched to simply "Justice." There was no separate toilet facility for the new woman justice, so O'Connor shared a restroom with female clerks down the hall from the justices' chambers. During her term in office, she endured treatment for breast cancer (and did not miss a day of oral arguments), and for the first twelve years she served as the lone woman on the Court. When Ruth Bader Ginsburg joined her on the bench in 1993, O'Connor welcomed her with enthusiasm. "It was a happy day indeed when [Ginsburg] was confirmed to join our Court," O'Connor wrote in her book *The Majesty of the Law*. The media had singled O'Connor out as the "woman justice," but with Ginsburg on the Court the two women were "treated just like the others," O'Connor noted with relief.

O'Connor served on the high court for twenty-four years, filling a role as moderator between the conservative and liberal wings. During her latter years, she was the swing vote on a number of issues, including abortion. She voted several times to preserve a woman's right to choose an abortion, provided the fifth vote in favor of college affirmative action programs, and voted with four other justices supporting rights for Americans imprisoned under antiterrorist laws. Observers referred to her as "the most powerful woman in America" because she often cast the deciding vote on the Court.

When she retired in 2005 to care for her ailing husband, President George W. Bush praised her as a "great
lady [who] rose above the obstacles of an earlier time and
became one of the most admired Americans of our time."
For her part, O'Connor revealed that she was "so sad" that
Bush had not replaced her with another woman justice.

antidiscrimination laws. The lawyer noted that the
Jaycees referred to new members as "customers" and
"solicited them in a way that business is solicited."

Justice O'Connor asked whether the Minnesota law
would force a group of blacks to admit white members if
their group had been formed to advocate causes for black
citizens. Varco replied that Minnesota's law probably
would not apply in such a case "if the admission of whites
to this black institution . . . could be shown to interfere
with some constitutionally protected freedom—let's say a
constitutionally protected right to hold a belief or to advocate a belief."

Justice Rehnquist offered another scenario: an Iranian
club, whose members proclaimed that "Iraq is all bad,"
forced to accept Iraqis. "If you admit enough Iraqis into
the Iranian society," Rehnquist theorized, "they're going
to quite substantially change the purpose of the organization."

Neither situation applied to the Jaycees' case, Varco
responded to the justices. "The difference between the . . .
cases," he said, "is that the issues that the Jaycees purport-
edly calls men's issues are not issues on which sex deter-
mines your point of view, . . . contrary of what happens in
the Iran/Iraq situation." The Jaycees, he noted, did not

require its members to hold any particular political points of view, and even if the organization had, a group of women would not necessarily all think differently from a group of men on the issues. Even if the Jaycees took a stand against the Equal Rights Amendment or women in the workforce, Varco noted, not all women would oppose that view and not all men would support it.

In his argument Varco took care to express his reverence for First Amendment protections. Several of the justices questioned him on whether the Minnesota law interfered with the Jaycees' free speech and other First Amendment rights. It did not, Varco assured them; rather, the First Amendment protected "certain private, intimate gatherings." The government, he said, "shouldn't be telling people who they have to go on picnics with." But that did not apply to the Jaycees, he said, "because the relationships that the people have [at Jaycees' meetings] are simply too impersonal and too commercial to be accorded any of those types of protection."

The justices asked Varco to list the characteristics that made the organization a business rather than a private club. In reply, Varco noted that the Jaycees was incorporated, that it charged for training sessions and other benefits, that its membership was open to large groups of people, and that the Jaycees' annual reports were similar to those issued by businesses. He noted that unlike private clubs that made money solely from dues, the Jaycees earned a good portion of its funds from the sales of merchandise, membership lists, and advertising in the club's magazine.

The justices questioned what made the Jaycees different from the Rotary Club or the Kiwanis, two organizations that also excluded women at the time. Varco replied that he knew little about either club, but he surmised that they were more selective in accepting members. Those organizations, he said, might be "more like the picnic among friends or the private club in which friendship or status gets you in. That simply isn't . . . true with respect to the Jaycees. Anybody [except women and older men] can get in." (Those clubs, too, would eventually open their doors to women.)

He concluded his remarks by reemphasizing that the Jaycees operated as a business. "I see very little difference," he told the Court, "between what the Jaycees do and how they operate and being able to go into a hotel with a dollar and get a room or a meal."

"Where can you go to a hotel for a dollar?" asked one of the justices. Laughter rippled through the courtroom.

"Not in this town, Your Honor," replied Varco.

That brought down the house, and the Court adjourned for lunch.

Jaycees' case

At 2:11 p.m. Carl Hall Jr. took his place before the Court. He immediately disputed Varco's claim that the Jaycees was a business. "It's a membership organization," he said, "substantially similar to hundreds of others in this country—Kiwanis, Lions, and others. . . . It's a young men's organization. Its purpose is to—essentially to assist young men in their development by means of community service."

A justice pointed out that the Jaycees differed from private organizations that voted members in. "[In] some of those organizations," the justice noted, "one vote can keep you out." Hall agreed that the Jaycees allowed any young man, not just those in business, to join the club. But, he argued, the Jaycees' broad membership policy should not "take away our right to free association."

The justices wanted to know how having women members would change the programs offered by the club. Hall said the programs might not change, but the acceptance of women members "would indeed change the internal [objectives], because the internal programs are directed to the self-improvement of just young men."

Justice White urged the lawyer to be specific. "What interests are there of young men that would be frustrated by having women members?"

"I think," answered Hall, "the desire of young men simply to have an organization that they entirely run and promotes solely their interest." He noted that the national membership had voted three times to continue the all-male policy.

The lawyer shifted his attention to the group's First Amendment claims, that the Minnesota law interfered with members' right to free speech. He noted that each year the group voted on a number of issues and took positions on community as well as national matters.

"Can you name me one position that applies only to men?" Justice Marshall pressed.

Hall acknowledged that he could not think of an issue that the members had voted on that applied only to men, "but I can foresee that . . . if they take a vote on ERA or the draft or abortion, or any of those sensitive issues, they could very well take a different position." That was not good enough for the justices, who returned to the question several times and pushed for specifics.

"You haven't identified one [position] yet" that would change if women were members, one justice said impatiently. "I've asked about it several times."

Hall suggested that the group might vote differently on abortion if women were among the members. But the justice noted that Hall had no idea how the male members would vote on the issue of abortion, observing that "All men don't agree on it [abortion]."

Justice Rehnquist drew smiles from those in the courtroom when he described a hypothetical organization "of male chauvinists that says we're tired of this affirmative action in favor of women." But, he told Hall, "You haven't really shown that the Jaycees . . . espouse anything close to men's rights or the kinds of issues that men and women might feel differently about."

Hall insisted that the group's "essential core purpose" was to advance young men's interests and that women would change that purpose. He noted that the club's male members learned to be effective executives by running projects developed by the Jaycees. His description of the Jaycees' training programs elicited a terse response from Justice O'Connor: "Women learn exactly the same way."

Hall responded that women could benefit from the training and noted that, as associates, several women did participate in Jaycees programs. But, he said, they had no right to vote or control policy.

"Well, tell me," Justice Marshall interjected, "what other right do they have, other than to pay their dues?" Again, the room erupted in laughter.

In another exchange, Hall argued that the Jaycees had "the basic fundamental right of freedom of association" to choose its own members. But one justice pointed out that when businesses have said they did not want to serve blacks, "this Court has said that the state's interest in eliminating discrimination is enough to put a stop to that."

Hall said again that the Jaycees was not a public accommodation, but the justice noted that businesses discriminating against blacks had made the same argument.

Hall made one last attempt to persuade the justices: noting that the law was vague, he said the Jaycees had no idea how to amend club bylaws to meet the law's requirements to qualify as a private club under the state's definition. With one minute of his allowable time remaining, Hall thanked the justices and sat down. At 2:41 p.m. Chief Justice Burger ended the session. The Jaycees, women, and Minnesota officials all waited to hear the justices' decision.

One of the many cartoons that dealt with the issues raised in the *Roberts* v. *Jaycees* case

eIGHT
JUDGMENT AND AFTERMATH

On JULY 3, 1984, THe COUrT delivered its unanimous decision that the Jaycees organization was required to open its doors to women members. In making the 7 to 0 ruling, the justices rejected the club's contention that First Amendment protections applied in the case. The Court also accepted Minnesota's definition of the organization as a public accommodation required to abide by the state's antidiscrimination laws.

Justice William J. Brennan Jr., author of the opinion, wrote that the Constitution protects people's right to pick their companions in two ways. First, a person's private choice of friends and associates is "a fundamental element of personal liberty." Second, the Constitution protects people's right to gather together to engage in activities protected by the First Amendment, such as practicing a religion, protesting, or speaking out on controversial issues.

Addressing the first category, Brennan noted the importance of close personal ties (for example, those among family members) and the role such bonds play in creating and preserving a nation's culture. "Protecting these relationships from unwarranted state interference therefore safeguards the ability independently to define one's identity that is central to any concept of liberty," Brennan wrote.

JUSTICE WILLIAM BRENNAN JR. WROTE THE UNANIMOUS DECISION IN *Roberts v. Jaycees*, WHICH OPENED THE CLUB'S MEMBERSHIP TO WOMEN.

But the justice put limits to this type of constitutional protection. He said that only certain types of relationships qualify under this principle. In general, only family relationships—those involving marriage, childbirth, the raising and education of children, and living with relatives, for example—and other close relationships can be granted privacy. These groups, Brennan continued, are marked by their small size, by the high degree of selectivity involved in becoming and remaining a member, and by the fact that "critical aspects" of the relationship are performed in private.

The Jaycees club did not meet such criteria, according to the opinion. "The undisputed facts reveal that the local chapters of the Jaycees are large and basically unselective groups," Brennan wrote. "Apart from age and sex, neither the national organization nor the local chapters employ any criteria for judging applicants for membership, and new members are routinely recruited and admitted with no inquiry into their backgrounds." He noted that the Minneapolis chapter had about 430 members and the St. Paul chapter had 400 members when the suit was initiated. Brennan also pointed out that, while women were not allowed to vote or hold office in the organization, they were permitted to pay to participate in training sessions, to assist with community projects, and to associate freely with the male members during these activities.

Free speech unaffected

Brennan then turned to the second instance in which the Constitution protects the right of association: if group members' free speech, or other First Amendment rights, would otherwise be threatened. The Jaycees had insisted that being forced to accept women members would jeopardize the male members' free speech. The Court, however, found that the club had not shown that the requirement imposed "any serious burdens on the male members' freedom of expressive association." The opinion rejected the "sexual stereotyping" behind the Jaycees' assertions that women as a group would vote differently on issues than men.

Moreover, Brennan wrote, Minnesota had good reason to require public groups not to discriminate. "By prohibiting gender discrimination in places of public accommodation, the Minnesota Act protects the . . . citizenry from a number of serious social and personal harms," the justice observed. "[D]iscrimination based on archaic and overbroad assumptions about the relative needs and capacities of the sexes forces individuals to labor under stereotypical notions that often bear no relationship to their actual abilities. It thereby both deprives persons of their individual dignity and denies society the benefits of wide participation in political, economic, and cultural life." Brennan added that those who were discriminated against because of their sex felt the sting of injustice just as strongly as those who received different treatment because of their race.

Finally, Brennan rejected the Jaycees' claim that Minnesota's antidiscrimination law was excessively vague and broad. He noted that in determining that the club fell under the law's requirements, the Minnesota Supreme Court had relied on "specific and objective criteria"—the Jaycees' size, how the group selected members, the club's "commercial nature," and its "use of public facilities." The law was not too broad, Brennan said, and noted the state supreme court's suggestion that some private groups, such as the Kiwanis, would not fall under the law's regulations. Unlike the Jaycees, the Kiwanis allowed members to join by invitation only and required them to meet specific qualifications.

Justices John Paul Stevens, Thurgood Marshall, Byron

White, and Lewis Powell joined Brennan's opinion. Justice Sandra Day O'Connor voted with the majority but supported the decision for different reasons, which she outlined in a concurring opinion. Justice William Rehnquist merely concurred with the judgment without explaining why he had not formally joined Brennan's opinion or written a concurrence. Chief Justice Warren Burger and Justice Harry Blackmun, both former members of the Minnesota Jaycees, did not participate in the vote.

In her concurrence, Justice O'Connor contended that the Court should not have even considered the Jaycees' claim of First Amendment rights because the organization was a commercial enterprise. "An association must choose its market," wrote O'Connor. "Once it enters the marketplace of commerce in any substantial degree it loses the complete control over its membership that it would otherwise enjoy if it confined its affairs to the marketplace of ideas." The Jaycees sold memberships, training programs, and a number of other products and services, all commercial activities, according to the justice.

To illustrate her point, Justice O'Connor noted that the Court had decided in an earlier case that a law firm could not restrict its partnerships to men. "As a commercial enterprise," she wrote, "the law firm could claim no First Amendment immunity from employment discrimination laws."

THE NEW JAYCEES

Those who had supported women's right to join the Jaycees' celebrated the Fourth of July the next day with extra zeal. Daniel Aberg, who had been president of the St. Paul chapter in 1978 when the national board took its action, greeted the ruling with relief that the battle was over "after six years of fighting. We can now go about our business without a cloud over us." Anne Ford Nelson, who in 1983 had served as the first woman president of the Community Business Leaders, hailed the decision. "I feel really vindicated," she told newspaper reporters. "When they said we could be associates, they said we can cook and do the grunt work but don't aspire." She was pleased that the Supreme Court had said that tomorrow's leaders would be women, too, "just like we always thought in St. Paul." Kristie Smith, a member of the St. Paul chapter, celebrated with fifty men and women after the ruling was delivered. "I didn't fight this issue as a woman, but as a business person," she said, "because I wanted to advance as a business person."

Minnesota's attorney general, Hubert H. Humphrey III, a key supporter of the women members' rights, said the Supreme Court decision established that "sex discrimination will not be accepted in the public marketplace."

In an editorial, the *New York Times* applauded the "sensible" ruling but observed that the Court had "a long way to go to resolve the churning conflict" between private clubs' claims of First Amendment rights and antidiscrimination laws. The editorial concluded by noting that "unless one believes men should use clubs to deprive women of business advantages," the ruling was fair.

While the ruling disappointed national Jaycees officials, they said they would comply with its directives. "The United States Jaycees has always believed in the U.S. court system that is defined by the Constitution and we will take the necessary steps to adhere to that system," national Jaycees president Tommy Todd told reporters. In August 1984 the club did just that, as national convention delegates voted overwhelmingly to admit women as full members of the organization. The vote marked the end of the Jaycees' twelve-year, million-dollar battle to keep women out of the club. A few Jaycees chapters closed down rather than admit women, and a few resisted the new policy in

DANIEL ABERG, FORMER PRESIDENT OF THE ST. PAUL JAYCEES, AND FORMER MEMBER COLLEEN O'KANE DISPLAY THE JULY 3, 1984, ISSUE OF THE *ST. PAUL DISPATCH*, WHICH REPORTED THE SUPREME COURT DECISION ORDERING THE JAYCEES TO OPEN MEMBERSHIP TO WOMEN.

RUTH Bader Ginsburg

On August 10, 1993, Ruth Bader Ginsburg, the second woman to serve as associate justice, joined Sandra Day O'Connor on the U.S. Supreme Court. In nominating Ginsburg, President Bill Clinton predicted that she would be "a great Justice" who would "move the Court not left or right but forward."

Her presence on the high court's bench made female justices a more routine phenomenon. While O'Connor's achievement was a "momentous" event, Ginsburg helped, in her words, "to make women's participation in all manners of legal work not 'momentous,' but 'commonplace.'"

Born in 1933, Ginsburg grew up in a poor, working-class neighborhood in Brooklyn, New York. Her parents named her Joan Ruth and called her Kiki. Her only sibling, a sister, died when Ginsburg was a toddler, and her mother died of cancer the day before her high school graduation. She received a scholarship to Cornell University and graduated first in her class. She married Martin Ginsburg, whom she had met at Cornell, and the couple moved to Oklahoma, where Martin Ginsburg served two years in the army.

The couple's next stop was Harvard Law School. Like O'Connor, Ginsburg faced strong resistance from men who believed that women should not practice law. The powerful administrators and professors at Harvard during the time promoted that view. Harvard did not provide dormitories for women, and Ginsburg—one of nine women in the law school class of 1959—lived with her husband and their young daughter off campus. All the professors were white men; the faculty club dining room barred women. "One could invite one's father, but not one's wife or mother, to the *Law Review* banquet," Ginsburg recalled in a speech at Harvard in 1998. Women were not allowed in the library's periodical room, and law firms that made use of the school's placement service hired only men. Only 3 percent of the law students were women; Harvard Business School did not accept women at all.

In addition to those indignities, professors as well as male students taunted the women in the class. Dean Erwin Griswold once asked his female students how they felt about filling seats that could have gone to worthy male students. The dean later singled out Ginsburg as "an outstanding example" of the lawyers "representing groups interested in the rights of women." Ginsburg credited Griswold's memo as playing a role in her appointment to the Supreme Court.

During the trying years at Harvard, Ginsburg faced a personal crisis as well, for her husband developed cancer. She cared for him, took notes in his law classes, typed his papers, and attended to their baby while maintaining her own course load and holding down a slot on the prestigious *Harvard Law Review*. Martin recovered and after graduation he accepted a job as an associate with a New York law firm. Ruth Bader Ginsburg transferred to Columbia Law School to be with him and became the first woman to serve on two law reviews when she won a spot on the Columbia journal.

After a year at Columbia Law, Ginsburg graduated at the top of her class. The doors that had been shut to O'Connor remained closed to Ginsburg a decade later. When law firms refused to hire her, Ginsburg took work that O'Connor had rejected—legal secretary. She went on to become the first woman to win tenure at Columbia as a professor of law. Beginning in the 1960s, Ginsburg worked as an advocate for women's rights. In 1972, the same year she won tenure, she became director of the Women's Rights Project operated by the American Civil Liberties Union. Later, as an ACLU lawyer, she argued six cases for women's rights before the Supreme Court, including the 1973 case *Frontiero* v. *Richardson*, in which the Court ruled that the air force could not discriminate against women when distributing benefits.

In 1981 President Jimmy Carter nominated Ginsburg to serve as a judge on the U.S. Court of Appeals in the District of Columbia Circuit, a post she held until being named to the Supreme Court.

As second woman on the bench, Ginsburg had a much smoother introduction to the Court than O'Connor had faced. By that time, much of the opposition to female justices had died down, a women's restroom had been installed in chambers, and most important, a woman stood ready to welcome her. Ginsburg said O'Connor played the role of "big sister" and "told me many things that made my life easier that first year." When the younger justice wrote her first Supreme Court opinion, on a complex dispute over pensions, O'Connor sent her a note of support, even though she was one of two justices to vote against the decision. The note said, "This is your first opinion for the Court. It is a fine opinion. I look forward to many more."

In the years that followed, Ginsburg has authored a number of major opinions that protect citizens' rights, among them *United States* v. *Virginia*. Writing for the majority in 1996, Ginsburg echoed the Court's words in *Frontiero*, the case she had argued decades earlier as an ACLU lawyer: "Our Nation has had a long and unfortunate history of sex discrimination." The ruling ordered Virginia Military Institute to open its doors to women. The government must act to protect women's rights to full citizenship, Ginsburg wrote, and those include "equal opportunity to aspire, achieve, participate in and contribute to society based on their individual talents and capacities."

Ginsburg's eloquent words had all the more meaning because she herself had suffered under restrictive policies and had endured to defeat such discrimination as justice on the highest court in the land, other ways. The San Antonio, Texas, chapter asked women applying for membership to participate in a swimsuit competition, while a male member in another Texas chapter told a reporter, "We'll allow women, but we're not comfortable about it."

Many other Jaycees chapters applauded the move. "Not being able to admit women has been a big problem for us," said Barry Kaufmann, president of the New York State Jaycees. "Everyone's real positive about [the Court's decision]." In Oak Grove, Georgia, members elected a woman president.

Women wasted little time in taking advantage of their new status in the organization. Kathleen Dugas was among the first to join the Nebraska Jaycees in 1984. Dugas had waited for months for the Supreme Court to issue its ruling on the *Roberts* case, preferring not to join until she could become a full member. "I thought it was discriminatory," she said of the Jaycees' all-men policy. "I wanted to be involved because I liked the projects they were doing." Ten years later, she was elected president of the Maine Junior Chamber of Commerce.

Christopher Beach, national press relations manager for the Jaycees in the 1990s, said in 1995 that the *Roberts* case "put us in step with the times. Men and women are now equal in business, it seems, and they're equal in the Jaycees." With members of both sexes, local chapters are "more reflecting of society."

In 2007, after another name change to the U.S. Junior Chamber, the organization had more than 170,000 members nationally, with chapters in eighty-eight countries. Women make up half of the present-day U.S. membership, and the age limit has been extended to forty. Past members include aviator Charles Lindbergh, presidents Bill Clinton and Gerald Ford, and basketball star Larry Bird. The organization continues to work on numerous community projects, including programs to help those affected by AIDS, an antismoking campaign aimed at children, and seminars and other educational programs to train young people in business.

Gains and Losses for Women's Rights

Three years after the *Roberts* decision, the Supreme Court extended its ruling to cover other clubs. In 1987 in *Board of Directors of Rotary International* v. *Rotary Club of Duarte*, the Court again ruled in a 7 to 0 vote that Rotary, a national nonprofit men's organization similar to the Jaycees, violated California law by barring women from membership. Justices O'Connor and Blackmun did not participate in that case. Following the ruling, the Rotary Club, Kiwanis International, and the Lions Club all opened their doors to women. The Boy Scouts, however, continues its all-male policy after winning lower court challenges. The U.S. Supreme Court has never ruled on the Scouts' exclusion of women and girls, but in a 2000 case, *Boy Scouts of America* v. *Dale*, the high court granted the group the right to bar gay men from leadership positions.

Another Supreme Court ruling, in *New York State Club Association* v. *City of New York*, put additional limits on all-male clubs. The decision, also in 1987, upheld a New York law forbidding discrimination against women and minorities by private clubs that had more than four hundred members, regularly served meals, and did business with the public.

A ruling in a more recent case extended protections against sex discrimination to the nation's military schools, bastions of male exclusivity since the 1800s. In *United States* v. *Virginia*, the issue was a claim by young women that Virginia Military Institute had discriminated against them by barring them from enrolling. The state of Virginia established a girls' version of the school to meet

JUSTICE RUTH BADER GINSBERG JOINED THE SUPREME COURT IN 1993, ONLY THE SECOND WOMAN TO HOLD THAT POST. IN 1996 SHE WROTE THE MAJORITY OPINION IN *UNITED STATES* V. *VIRGINIA*, WHICH REQUIRED VIRGINIA MILITARY INSTITUTE TO ACCEPT FEMALE CADETS.

constitutional objections, but the Supreme Court rejected that plan. Justice Ruth Bader Ginsburg delivered the 7 to 1 opinion. In writing the opinion, Ginsburg quoted the Court's ruling in the *Frontiero* case she had argued more than two decades earlier: "Our Nation has had a long and

sexual Harassment on the job

In March 1975 Lois Jenson took advantage of a new effort by the federal government to open nontraditional jobs to women: she began working at the Eveleth Mines in northern Minnesota. The job was arduous—cleaning soot from the huge mining machinery—but the abuse from fellow workers proved much harder to bear.

Some men at the mines, including managers, subjected the women workers to brutal sexual abuse and harassment. Many of the male workers believed women should not take "men's jobs" but should stay at home as wives and mothers or work in positions traditionally held by women. The abusers drew obscene pictures and sexual graffiti on the walls of the lunchroom, the women's locker room and restrooms, the offices, and the elevators. The women found obscene posters on their cars and in their lockers. Male workers pushed over a portable toilet at a job site while a woman was using it. Men groped women, pinched them, grabbed them, and called them lewd names as they walked by. One woman told of semen smeared on the clothing she kept in her locker. Some women feared for their lives, according to a steelworkers union official who tried to help the women at the mine where he also worked.

Despite state and federal laws banning sexual harassment on the job, company officials ignored the abuse. When the women, no longer able to endure the harassment, finally complained, the officials refused to do anything to stop the harassment or punish the harassers.

After nine years on the job, Jenson filed a complaint with the Minnesota Department of Human Rights. She decided to take the action when the company took no action to protect her from a male coworker who was stalking her. In January 1987 the state department found probable cause and asked the company to pay Jenson $11,000 in damages. Eveleth refused to pay. Jenson contacted dozens of lawyers, but no one would represent her. At last, however, Paul Sprenger, a Minnesota lawyer with experience in employment discrimination, agreed to take the case. In 1988 Sprenger filed suit against the mining company in district court. Three years later the court granted the lawsuit class-action status and expanded it to cover other women employed at the mine. Two women joined the historic suit, but other female mine workers, fearful of retribution, signed a petition denying that any sexual harassment had taken place. Eventually, twenty-one women participated in the suit, including some who had initially signed the petition.

In 1993 the court ruled that the company should have stopped the harassment and ordered a trial to determine how much the mine should pay in damages. At the trial, overseen by a retired male judge, company lawyers scrutinized the women's private lives in an effort to prove the women had "asked for" the harassment. In the end, however, the Eighth Circuit Court of Appeals overruled the judge's meager award of $10,000 for each plaintiff. In 1998, fourteen years after Jenson filed her initial complaint, Eveleth agreed to settle for $3.5 million to avoid a jury trial. Jenson, as well as another woman worker, eventually had to leave her job in the mine after being diagnosed with posttraumatic stress disorder.

The case established a precedent in sexual harassment law. As a result of the outcome, businesses began to take sexual harassment seriously. Today companies throughout the United States have adopted policies to identify and prevent the problem, routinely training workers on the issue, and setting up systems to respond to complaints of sexual harassment.

unfortunate history of sex discrimination." It is fine, she noted, to celebrate the "inherent differences" between men and women, but those differences should not be used for "denigration of the members of either sex" or to limit people's opportunities. Classifications based on sex, she observed, "may not be used, as they once were, . . . to create or perpetuate the legal, social, and economic inferiority of women."

During the years following the *Jaycees* case, women made enormous strides in some areas. Sally Ride became the first woman astronaut to travel to space in 1983; several other women followed, including Eileen Marie Collins, the first woman to pilot a space shuttle. In the political arena, women won seats in local, regional, and national elections. A 1991 case, *International Union* v. *Johnson Controls Inc.*, opened new opportunities for young women when the Court overturned the 1908 *Muller* decision, which limited work conditions and higher-paying jobs for women who might be pregnant. "Fertile women, as far as appears in the record, participate in the manufacture of batteries as efficiently as anyone else," Justice Blackmun noted in his majority opinion.

In business, as in other areas, women posted both gains and losses. Under the Equal Employment Opportunity Act of 1972, businesses were required to set up affirmative action programs to open more top-level jobs to women and minorities. But during the 1980s, under pressure from business interests, President Ronald Reagan worked to broaden exemptions to the programs. Those efforts resulted in the elimination of affirmative action programs by more than 70 percent of government contractors. Many had looked at such programs with suspicion, claiming that they discriminated against white males. In a 1995 case, *Adarand Constructors* v. *Pena*, the Supreme Court placed tough new limits on affirmative action programs. Under the ruling, minorities and women had to prove a history of discrimination in order to win preferential treatment under the programs.

Congress added teeth to Title VII with the Civil Rights Act of 1991, giving victims of discrimination the right to collect money and to demand a trial by jury for their grievances. But in a 1993 case, *St. Mary's Honor Center* v. *Hicks*, the Supreme Court placed additional burdens on those charging discrimination. In a 5 to 4 decision, the Court ruled that plaintiffs had to show not only that the employer had lied about their dismissal but also that the discrimination against them had been on purpose.

women in today's workforce

The early feminists might well be amazed at women's progress. The role of women in society has changed dramatically. Women no longer are legally required to turn over their possessions and their earnings to the men they marry. They can work at jobs from astronaut to welder to business executive. They can practice law, serve on juries, and judge cases; they can have their own credit rating, run for political office, and own businesses. Women have made great strides in politics, business, and other fields.

In the past two decades a record number of women have held high political positions. President Bill Clinton named several women to his cabinet and other high-level posts: Madeleine Albright became the first woman to serve as secretary of state and went on to become U.S ambassador to the United Nations, Donna Shalala was appointed secretary of Health and Human Services, Janet Reno served as attorney general, Hazel O'Leary was named secretary of the Department of Energy, and Carol Browner held the top post at the Environmental Protection Agency. Clinton's appointment of Ruth Bader Ginsburg brought a second woman to the Supreme Court.

Condoleezza Rice took office as secretary of state under President George W. Bush in 2005. In the Senate, Democrat Carol Moseley Braun of Illinois took her seat in 1993, the first black woman to be elected to that body. Nancy Pelosi, elected Speaker of the House of Representatives in 2007, is the first woman to achieve that honor. Senator Hillary Clinton ran a strong campaign in her quest to become the first woman president.

Women have made similar advances in business. At the beginning of the twenty-first century, working women have become the norm. They make up almost 50 percent of the workforce, hold more than 40 percent of the nation's managerial positions, and comprise 23 percent of all chief executive officers. In 2007 women were CEOs at PepsiCo., Xerox, eBay, Kraft Foods, Archer Daniels Midland, Time Inc., Viacom, Sara Lee, Avon Products, and Procter & Gamble. Billionaire Oprah Winfrey headed her own multimedia empire, starred in and produced her own top-rated TV talk show, created other shows and a TV network, and founded and published a popular national magazine.

Federal laws prohibit unequal treatment on the job, and other laws protect women against sexual harassment at work. The percentage of women on the boards of the nation's top five hundred businesses has grown from 9.6 percent to 14.6 percent.

But there are still battles to be won: lifting women out of poverty, working to upgrade women's pay, breaking the glass ceiling that keeps many women from the most prestigious jobs. In 1984, when the Court issued its decision against the Jaycees, women who worked at full-time jobs earned about 67.8 percent of what male workers were paid, according to the CRS, a research arm of the Library of Congress. Women workers in 2007 still received less than their male counterparts: from 76 to 81 cents for every dollar earned by men in the workforce. Only 2 percent of the CEOs of Fortune 500 companies were women. And in 2007 forty-five of the top five hundred businesses, including National Semiconductor and financial services company Bear Stearns, had no women at all on their boards. In 2008 Apple Computer appointed Andrea Jung, chairman and CEO of Avon Products, to its previously all-male board.

The push to get equal pay has been complicated by the choice of many women to have children and work part-time or avoid overtime, for at least some of their business career. "People who do best in a field (financially) just plain put in more hours," says Warren Farrell, author of a book on the pay gap and a former board member of the New York City chapter of the National Organization for Women. Women's choices to work fewer hours, select lower-paying jobs, and reject jobs that entail danger or travel explain in part the discrepancy between women's pay and men's pay.

But observers believe that discrimination against women in the workforce remains. Heidi Hartmann, president of the Institute for Women's Policy Research, estimates that discrimination accounts for between 25 and 33 percent of cases in which men receive higher pay than women.

Even with such mixed results, work has been for many women the most effective path to equality. "Women have advanced extraordinarily in the workplace in the last decades," says Alice Eagly, professor of psychology at Northwestern University and coauthor of a book on women's challenges in attaining leadership roles. The world of business continues to change, and male workers, too, have begun to seek more time with their families. There are more opportunities for women in business, and more employers are adopting flexible work schedules, on-site child care, and other schemes to help parents of both sexes juggle family and career.

Although discrimination against women still exists in American society, people today have an arsenal of tools to combat it. State and federal laws, equal opportunity boards, federal and business policy, and court cases such as *Roberts* v. *U.S. Jaycees* all offer avenues to address and remedy instances of discrimination. Perhaps the best tool of all, however, is public opinion. During a celebration of International Women's Day in 2002, the remarks of then Secretary of State Colin Powell signified the enormous change in attitude of public officials on the importance of women's rights from the days when John Adams mocked his wife's insistence to "Remember the Ladies":

> Women's issues affect not only women; they have profound implications for all humankind. Women's issues are human rights issues. We, as a world community, cannot even begin to tackle the array of problems and challenges confronting us without the full and equal participation of women in all aspects of life.

NOTES

Chapter 1

p. 9, par. 2; p.11, par. 2, Findings of Fact, Conclusions of Law and Order, *State of Minnesota* v. *The United States Jaycees*, Office of Hearing Examiners, Department of Human Rights, October 9, 1979.

p. 12, par. 1, "A History of the USJC," U.S. Junior Chamber Web site, http://www.usjaycees.org/history.htm

p. 13, par. 2, Ralph Nader, "Opening Jaycee Doors to Women," *In the Public Interest*, June 25, 1972.

p. 15, par. 2, "Oust Women?" *Time*, September 4, 1978, http://www.time.com/time/magazine/article/0,9171,91 2125,00.html

p. 16, par. 3, *Bradwell* v. *State of Illinois*, 83 U.S. 130 (1873).

Chapter 2

p. 20, par. 1, *Bradwell* v. *State of Illinois*, 83 U.S. 130 (1873). Letter from Abigail Adams to John Adams, March 31, 1776 [electronic edition]. *Adams Family Papers: An Electronic Archive*. Massachusetts Historical Society, http://www.masshist.org/digitaladams/aea/

p. 20, par. 2, Letter from John Adams to Abigail Adams, April 4, 1776 [electronic edition]. *Adams Family Papers*. http://www.masshist.org/digitaladams/

p. 20, par. 3, Letter from Thomas Jefferson to Samuel

Kercheval, 1816. *The Writings of Thomas Jefferson, Memorial Edition* (Lipscomb and Bergh, eds.), Washington, D.C., 1903–1904. University of Virginia Library, Digital Collections Web site, http://etext.virginia.edu/jefferson/quotations/jeff1100.htm

p. 21, par. 1, "Women's History in America," Women's International Center, http://www.wic.org/misc/history.htm

p. 23, par. 2, Declaration of Sentiments (from Stanton, E. C, *A History of Woman Suffrage*, vol. 1, Rochester, NY, Fowler and Wells, 1889), 70–71), http://www.rochester.edu/SBA/declare.html

p. 23, par. 4, Jules Archer, *Breaking Barriers: The Feminist Revolution from Susan B. Anthony to Margaret Sanger to Betty Friedan*, New York: Viking, 1991, 35–36.

p. 26, par. 3, Elizabeth Cady Stanton, "A Slave's Appeal," address to the Judiciary Committee of the New York State Legislature, March 1860.

p. 28, par. 1, quoted in Otto Friedrich, "Braving Scorn and Threats, *Time*, July 23, 1984.

p. 28, par. 2, "Obituary of Elizabeth Cady Stanton," *New York Times*, October 27, 1902.

p. 29, par. 2, *Bradwell v. State of Illinois*, 83 U.S. 130 (1873), concurrence, Justice Joseph P. Bradley.

p. 30, par. 1, quoted in Archer, *Breaking Barriers*, p. 69.

p. 32, par. 2, "Suffrage Wins in Senate; Now Goes to States," *New York Times*, June 5, 1919, 1.

p. 32, par. 5, quoted in "Woman Suffrage Amendment Wins in Legislature: Unanimous Vote Is Given for It in Senate and Assembly," *New York Times*, June 17, 1919, 1.

p. 33, par. 1, quoted in Hugh Mallory, "Two Amendments; South, Up in Arms against Suffrage, Raises Prohibition Question," *New York Times*, June 20, 1919, 12.

p. 35, par. 2, "Tennessee Completes Suffrage Victory," *New York Times*, August 19, 1920, 1.

p. 35, par. 3 (sentence 2), Kate Soulier, "Historical Perspective: Does One Vote Count?" *Earlybird*, issue 13,
May 25, 2004, http://www.utahpolicy.com/pages/
newsletters/Issue13.htm

p. 35, par. 3, quoted in Paula Casey, "A Legacy of Leadership: Tennessee's Pivotal Role in Granting All American
Women the Vote," commencement address, 1995,
http://gos.sbc.edu/c/casey.html

Chapter 3

p. 37, par. 2, quoted in "Coolidge Assures Women of Victory," *New York Times*, November 18, 1923.

p. 38, par. 3, *Muller* v. *Oregon*, 208 U.S. 412 (1908).

p. 39, par. 2, Sheridan Harvey, "Rosie the Riveter: Real
Women Workers in World War II," *Journeys & Crossings*,
Library of Congress, http://www.loc.gov/rr/program/
journey/rosie-transcript.html

p. 41, par. 1, "Women in War Jobs—Rosie the Riveter
(1942–1945)," Historic Campaigns, Ad Council Web
site, http://www.adcouncil.org/default.aspx?id=128

p. 41, par. 3, Harvey, "Rosie the Riveter."

p. 41, par. 4–p. 42, par. 1, quoted in Harvey, "Rosie the
Riveter."

p. 42, par. 4–p. 43, par. 1, quoted in Bess Furman, "Senate
to Vote on Equal Rights," *New York Times*, July 19, 1946,
11.

p. 43, par. 3, Bess Furman, "Equal Rights Fails to Get
Two-thirds in Vote in Senate," *New York Times*, July 20,
1946, 1.

p. 43, par. 4, "The Sisters of Abigail Adams." *Time*, February 6, 1950.

p. 44, par. 4, Eileen Shanahan, "Equal Rights Amendment
Is Approved by Congress," *New York Times*, March 23,
1972, 1.

Chapter 4

p. 49, par. 2, "Anne R. Davidow," Michigan Supreme Court Historical Society Web site, http://www.micourt history.org/resources/women-and-law/davidow.php

p. 50, par. 2, Jules Archer, *Breaking Barriers: The Feminist Revolution from Susan B. Anthony to Margaret Sanger to Betty Friedan*, New York: Viking, 1991, 137–138.

p. 50, par. 3, Toni Carabillo et al., eds., *Feminist Chronicles: 1953–1993*, Los Angeles: Women's Graphics, 1993, 7.

p. 54, par. 2, quoted in Flora Davis, *Moving the Mountain: The Women's Movement in America Since 1960*, New York: Simon & Schuster, 1991, p. 42.

p. 54, par. 3, quoted in Davis, *Moving the Mountain*, 43.

p. 55, par. 1, 2, Jo Freeman, Ph.D., "How 'Sex' Got into Title VII: Persistent Opportunism as a Maker of Public Policy," *Law and Inequality: A Journal of Theory and Practice*, vol. 9, no. 2, March 1991, pp. 163–184.

p. 57, par. 2, quoted in Carabillo et al., eds., *Feminist Chronicles*, 18.

p. 58, par. 2, "The Founding of NOW," NOW Web site, http://www.now.org/history/the_founding.html

p. 58, par. 3–p. 59, par. 1, "The National Organization for Women's 1966 Statement of Purpose," NOW Web site, http://www.now.org/history/purpos66.html

p. 61, par. 1, *Pittsburgh Press Company* v. *Pittsburgh Commission on Human Relations*, 413 U.S. 376 (1973).

p. 61, par. 2, Equal Employment Opportunity Act of 1972, U.S. Equal Employment Opportunity Commission, Web site http://www.eeoc.gov/abouteeoc/35th/thelaw/index.html

p. 62, par. 2, Oyez Project, *Reed* v. *Reed*, 404 U.S. 71 (1971).

p. 63, par. 2, Oyez Project, *Personnel Administrator of Massachusetts* v. *Feeney*, 442 U.S. 256 (1979).

Chapter 5

p. 65, par. 2, "A History of Minnesota Department of Human Rights," MDHR Web site, http://www.human rights.state.mn.us/about_history.html

p. 65, par. 2 (1955 law), Minnesota Statute 363A.02 Subd. 1 (5)(b).

p. 68, par. 2, record of hearing examiner's ruling, *Roberts* v. *U.S. Jaycees* case file, No. 83-724, A-121.

p. 68, par. 4, quoted in appellant's brief, *Roberts* v. *U.S. Jaycees* case file, No. 83-724, 22.

p. 69, par. 3, quoted in record of U.S. District Court's ruling, *Roberts* v. *U.S. Jaycees* case file, No. 83-724, p. A-133.

p. 70, par. 2, quoted in appellant's brief, *Roberts* v. *U.S. Jaycees* case file, No. 83-724, 3.

p. 70, par. 3–p. 71, par. 1, *U.S. Power Squadrons* v. *State Human Rights Appeals Board*, 59 N.Y.2d 401, 410-11, 452 N.E.2d 1199, 1203, 465 N.Y.S.2d 871, 875 (1983).

p. 71, par. 3, Dennis Hevesi, "Donald P. Lay, 80, Federal Judge Notable in Rights Cases, Dies," *New York Times*, May 2, 2007.

Chapter 6

pp. 76–78, Supreme Court Historical Society, http://www.supremecourthistory.org; Administrative Office of the U.S. Courts, http://www.uscourts.gov; Iowa Court Information System, http://www.judicial.state.ia.us/students/6 [site contains diagram].

p. 79, par. 3–p.81, par. 1, appellant's brief, *Roberts* v. *U.S. Jaycees* case file.

p. 81, par. 2–p. 82, par. 1, respondent's brief, *Roberts* v. *U.S. Jaycees* case file.

p.82, par. 2, appellant's reply brief, *Roberts* v. *U.S. Jaycees* case file.

p. 82, par. 3–p. 83, par. 1, motion of Northwestern Bell

Telephone Company for leave to file amicus brief, *Roberts* v. *U.S. Jaycees* case file.

p. 83, par. 2, amicus brief for National Organization for Women et al., *Roberts* v. *U.S. Jaycees* case file, p. 18.

p. 83, par. 3–84, par. 1, amicus brief for Boys Scouts of America, *Roberts* v. *U.S. Jaycees* case file, 4.

Chapter 7

p. 85, par. 2; p. 86, par. 1, quoted in Tony Mauro, "Speak Wisely: Those Who Dare to Take the Podium at the Supreme Court Best Come Prepared," *American Lawyer*, September 7, 2004, http://www.law.com/jsp/article.jsp?id=1094073214030

p. 86, par. 3, *Minneapolis Star & Tribune*, July 4, 1984, at 10A, col. 4. Cited in "Freedom of Association after *Roberts* v. *United States Jaycees*," Douglas O. Linder, *Michigan Law Review*, August 1984.

p. 89, par. 2–3; p. 93, par. 1–p. 95, par. 4, Richard L. Varco Jr., oral arguments, *Roberts* v. *United States Jaycees*, 468 U.S. 609 (1984), http://www.oyez.org/cases/1980-1989/1983/1983_83_724/argument

pp. 90–93, Supreme Court Historical Society, "Sandra Day O'Connor," http://www.supremecourthistory.org; Tony Mauro, "Law's Smallest Club: Ruth Bader Ginsburg and Sandra Day O'Connor Are Polar Opposites with Abiding Bonds," *The American Lawyer*, June 12, 2003; The Oyez Project, "Sandra Day O'Connor," http://www.oyez.org/justices/sandra_day_oconnor; Warren Richey, "Sandra Day O'Connor Announces Retirement," *Christian Science Monitor*, July 1, 2005.

p. 95, par. 6–p. 97, par. 7, Carl D. Hall Jr., oral arguments, *Roberts* v. *United States Jaycees*, 468 U.S. 609 (1984), http://www.oyez.org/cases/1980-1989/1983/1983_83_724/argument

Chapter 8

p. 99, par. 2–3; p. 101, par. 1–p. 102, par. 3, *Roberts* v. *United States Jaycees*, 468 U.S. 609 (1984).

p. 103, par. 2–3, *Roberts* v. *United States Jaycees*, Justice Sandra Day O'Connor, concurrence.

p. 103, par. 4–p. 104, par. 1 (Nelson, first quote), quoted in "Those Who Sued Jaycees on Bias Celebrate," *New York Times*, July 5, 1984.

p. 104, par. 1 (Nelson, second quote), Associated Press, "Winners Hail Ruling," *New York Times*, July 4, 1984, 1.

p. 104, par. 1 (Smith), "Those Who Sued Jaycees on Bias Celebrate."

p. 104, par. 2, Associated Press, "Winners Hail Ruling."

p. 104, par. 3, "Not for Men Only," *New York Times*, July 6, 1984, op-ed page.

p. 104, par. 4, Associated Press, "Winners Hail Ruling."

pp. 106–108, Joan Biskupic, "Ginsburg 'Lonely' without O'Connor," *USA Today*, January 26, 2007, p. 1A; Justice Ruth Bader Ginsberg, Speech at Celebration 45 at Harvard Law School on November 14, 1998 (updated for Celebration 50), *Harvard Journal of Law & Gender*, vol. 28, Spring 2005; Linda Greenhouse, "Senate, 96–3, Easily Affirms Judge Ginsburg as a Justice," *New York Times*, August 4, 1993; Tony Mauro, "Law's Smallest Club: Ruth Bader Ginsburg and Sandra Day O'Connor Are Polar Opposites with Abiding Bonds," *The American Lawyer*, June 12, 2003; The Oyez Project, "Ruth Bader Ginsburg," http://www.oyez.org/justices/ruth_bader ginsburg; Warren Richey, "Sandra Day O'Connor Announces Retirement," *Christian Science Monitor*, July 1, 2005; Mark Sherman, "Ginsburg Only Woman on High Court," Associated Press, June 4, 2007; Supreme Court Historical Society, "Ruth Bader Ginsburg." http://www.supremecourthistory.org

p. 109, par. 1–2, "Some Units of Jaycees Rebel against Admitting Women," *New York Times*, Sept. 10, 1984, A-14.

p. 109, par. 3, Interview with Kathleen Dugas by author, May 30, 1995.

p. 109, par. 4, Interview with Christopher Beach by author, May 30, 1995.

p. 111, par. 1; p. 114, par. 1, *United States* v. *Virginia*, 518 U.S. 515 (1996).

pp. 112–113, Niki Caro, director, *North Country*, Warner Brothers, 2005 (movie); Stephanie Hemphill, "Movie Stirs Memories on Iron Range," Minnesota Public Radio, January 28, 2005; Hemphill, "'North Country' Premieres on the Iron Range," Minnesota Public Radio, October 15, 2005; *"Jenson* vs. *Eveleth Mines*, Sexual Harassment in the Workplace," Sexual Harassment Support Group Web site, http://www.sexualharassmentsupport.org/JensonVs EvelethMines.html; *Lois E. Jenson et al* v. *Eveleth Taconite Company*, United States Court of Appeals for the Eighth Circuit, No., 97-1147, filed December 5, 1997.

p. 114, par. 2, *International Union* v. *Johnson Controls Inc.*, 499 U.S. 187 (1991).

p. 114, par. 3, Flora Davis, *Moving the Mountain: The Women's Movement in America Since 1960*, New York: Simon & Schuster, 1991, 440.

p. 116, par. 2, Katie Benner, Eugenia Levenson, and Rupali Arora, "50 Most Powerful Women 2007," *Fortune* at CNNMoney.com, http://money.cnn.com/magazines/ fortune/mostpowerfulwomen/2007

p. 116, par. 3, Carol Loomis, "Getting Women to the Highest Levels," *Fortune* at CNNMoney.com, http:// money.cnn.com/2007/10/04/magazines/fortune/ loomis_boards.fortune/index.htm

p. 116, par. 4 (CRS), Charles V. Dale and Linda Levine, "RL30902: Pay Equity Legislation in the 107th Congress," *CRS Report for Congress*, March 26, 2001, http://

www.cnie.org/NLE/CRSreports/Economics/econ-109.
cfm

p. 116, par. 4, Deborah Amos, "Women's Perks Can Bring
New Problems," *Morning Edition*, National Public Radio,
October 10, 2007.

p. 117, par. 1, "Women on Boards (Not!)," *Fortune* at CNN-
Money.com, http://money.cnn.com/magazines/fortune
/fortune_archive/2007/10/15/100536852/index.htm

p. 117, par. 2, Jeanne Sahadi, "Where Women's Pay Trumps
Men's," *Everyday Money*, CNNMoney.com, http://
money.cnn.com/2006/02/28/commentary/everyday/
sahadi/index.htm

p. 117, par. 3, Cited in Jeanne Sahadi, "The 76-cent Myth,"
Everyday Money, CNNMoney.com, http://money.cnn.
com/2006/02/21/commentary/everyday/sahadi/index.
htm

p. 117, par. 4, Quoted in Amos, "Women's Perks Can Bring
New Problems."

p. 118, par. 2, Secretary of State Colin Powell, remarks at
the meeting with women's organizations, White House,
November 19, 2001.

All Web sites accessible as of October 12, 2007.

furtHer information

BOOKS

Adams, Colleen. *Women's Suffrage: A Primary Source History of the Women's Rights Movement in America* (Primary Sources in American History). New York: Rosen Publishing Group, 2002.

Banks, Joan. *The U.S. Constitution, Your Government: How It Works*. Broomall, PA: Chelsea House, 2001.

Bausum, Ann. *With Courage and Cloth: Winning the Fight for a Woman's Right to Vote*. Washington, DC: National Geographic Children's Books, 2004.

Bohannon, Lisa Frederiksen. *Women's Rights and Nothing Less: The Story of Elizabeth Cady Stanton* (Feminist Voices). Greensboro, NC: Morgan Reynolds, 2000.

Cornelius, Kay. *The Supreme Court, Your Government: How It Works*. Broomall, PA.: Chelsea House, 2000.

Kendall, Martha. *Failure Is Impossible!: The History of American Women's Rights* (People's History). Minneapolis, MN: Lerner Group, 2001.

Mountjoy, Shane. *The Women's Rights Movement: Moving*

Toward Equality (Social and Political Reform Movements in American History). Broomall, PA: Chelsea House, 2007.

Patrick, John J. *The Supreme Court of the United States: A Student Companion* (Oxford Student Companions to American Government), 2nd ed. New York: Oxford University Press Children's Books, 2002.

VIDEOTAPES/FILMS
Burns, Ken. *Not for Ourselves Alone*, PBS, 1999 (video).

Caro, Niki. director. *North Country*, Warner Brothers, 2005 (film).

Cooney, Robert P. J. Jr., director. *Winning the Vote: The Triumph of the American Woman Suffrage Movement*, American Graphic, 2005 (video).

Generations: American Women Win the Vote, Vote 70, Inc., 2003 (video).

One Woman, One Vote, "The American Experience," PBS, 1995 (video).

von Garnier, Katja, director. *Iron Jawed Angels*, Warner Home Video, 2004 (video).

WEB SITES
Cornell University Law School (Supreme Court collection)
http://www.law.cornell.edu/supct/

FindLaw (U.S. Supreme Court Cases)
http://www.findlaw.com/casecode/supreme.html

First Amendment Center
http://www.firstamendmentcenter.org

Legal Information Institute, Cornell Law School
http://www.law.cornell.edu

Library of Congress, American Memory section
http://memory.loc.gov/ammem/collections/continental

National Archives, original documents
http://www.archives.gov

Oyez Project: U.S. Supreme Court multimedia Web site
http://www.oyez.org

Supreme Court Historical Society.
http://www.supremecourthistory.org

Supreme Court of the United States
http://www.supremecourtus.gov

All Web sites accessible as of October 12, 2007.

BIBLIOGRAPHY

CONSTITUTIONAL AMENDMENTS; FEDERAL AND STATE
  STATUTES
Amendment XIII
Amendment XIV
Amendment XV
Amendment XIX (Susan B. Anthony Amendment)
Civil Rights Act of 1964
Equal Employment Opportunity Act of 1972
Equal Pay Act (1965)
Equal Rights Amendment (Proposed)
Minnesota Act Against Discrimination (1969)
Minnesota Human Rights Act (1980 and 1982)
Title VII of the Civil Rights Act of 1964

ARTICLES
Amos, Deborah. "Women's Perks Can Bring New Prob-
    lems." *Morning Edition*, National Public Radio,
    October 10, 2007.
"Anne R. Davidow." Michigan Supreme Court Historical
    Society Web site, http://www.micourthistory.org/
    resources/women-and-law/davidow.php
Associated Press. "Winners Hail Ruling." *New York Times*,
    July 4, 1984, 1.
Benner, Katie, Eugenia Levenson, and Rupali Arora. "50
    Most Powerful Women 2007." *Fortune* at CNNMoney.

com, http://money.cnn.com/magazines/fortune/most powerfulwomen/2007

Biskupic, Joan. "Ginsburg 'Lonely' without O'Connor," *USA Today*, January 26, 2007, 1A.

Casey, Paula. "A Legacy of Leadership: Tennessee's Pivotal Role in Granting All American Women the Vote." Commencement address, 1995. http://gos.sbc.edu/c/casey.html

"Coolidge Assures Women of Victory." *New York Times*, November 18, 1923.

Dale, Charles V., and Linda Levine. "RL30902: Pay Equity Legislation in the 107th Congress." *CRS Report for Congress*, March 26, 2001, http://www.cnie.org/NLE/CRS reports/Economics/econ-109.cfm

"The Founding of NOW." NOW Web site, http://www.now.org/history/the_founding.html

Freeman, Jo. "How 'Sex' Got into Title VII: Persistent Opportunism as a Maker of Public Policy." *Law and Inequality: A Journal of Theory and Practice*, vol. 9: no. 2, March 1991, pp. 163–184.

Friedrich, Otto. "Braving Scorn and Threats." *Time*, July 23, 1984.

Furman, Bess. "Equal Rights Fails to Get Two-thirds in Vote in Senate." *New York Times*, July 20, 1946, 1.

———. "Senate to Vote on Equal Rights." *New York Times*, July 19, 1946, 11.

Ginsberg, Ruth Bader. Speech at Celebration 45 at Harvard Law School, November 14, 1998 (updated for Celebration 50), *Harvard Journal of Law & Gender*, vol. 28, spring 2005.

Greenhouse, Linda. "Senate, 96–3, Easily Affirms Judge Ginsburg as a Justice," *New York Times*, August 4, 1993.

Harvey, Sheridan. "Rosie the Riveter: Real Women Workers in World War II." *Journeys & Crossings*, Library of Congress. http://www.loc.gov/rr/program/journey/

rosie-transcript.html

Hemphill, Stephanie, "Movie Stirs Memories on Iron Range," Minnesota Public Radio, January 28, 2005.

———. "'North Country' Premieres on the Iron Range," Minnesota Public Radio, October 15, 2005.

Hevesi, Dennis. "Donald P. Lay, 80, Federal Judge Notable in Rights Cases, Dies." *New York Times*, May 2, 2007.

"A History of Minnesota Department of Human Rights." MDHR Web site. http://www.humanrights.state.mn.us/about_history.html

"A History of the USJC." U.S. Junior Chamber Web site, http://www.usjaycees.org/history.htm

Interview with Christopher Beach by author, May 30, 1995.

Interview with Kathleen Dugas by author, May 30, 1995.

Letter from Abigail Adams to John Adams, March 31, 1776 [electronic edition]. *Adams Family Papers: An Electronic Archive.* Massachusetts Historical Society, http://www.masshist.org/digitaladams

Letter from John Adams to Abigail Adams, 4 April 1776 [electronic edition]. *Adams Family Papers: An Electronic Archive.* Massachusetts Historical Society. http://www.masshist.org/digitaladams/

Letter from Thomas Jefferson to Samuel Kercheval, 1816. *The Writings of Thomas Jefferson, Memorial Edition* (Lipscomb and Bergh, eds.), Washington, DC: 1903–1904. University of Virginia Library, Digital Collections site. http://etext.virginia.edu/jefferson/quotations/jeff1100.htm

Linder, Douglas O. "Freedom of Association after *Roberts* v. *United States Jaycees*." *Michigan Law Review*, August 1984.

Loomis, Carol. "Getting Women to the Highest Levels." *Fortune* at CNNMoney.com, http://money.cnn.com/2007/10/04/magazines/fortune/loomis_boards.fortune/index.htm

Mallory, Hugh. "Two Amendments; South, Up in Arms

Against Suffrage, Raises Prohibition Question," *New York Times*, June 20, 1919, 12.

Mauro, Tony. "Law's Smallest Club: Ruth Bader Ginsburg and Sandra Day O'Connor Are Polar Opposites with Abiding Bonds." *American Lawyer*, June 12, 2003.

——. "Speak Wisely: Those Who Dare to Take the Podium at the Supreme Court Best Come Prepared." *American Lawyer*, September 7, 2004. http://www. law.com/jsp/article.jsp?id=1094073214030

Nader, Ralph. "Opening Jaycee Doors to Women." *In the Public Interest*, June 25, 1972.

"The National Organization for Women's 1966 Statement of Purpose." NOW Web site, http://www.now.org/history/purpos66.html

"Not for Men Only." *New York Times*, July 6, 1984.

Obituary of Elizabeth Cady Stanton. *New York Times*, October 27, 1902.

"Oust Women?" *Time*, September 4, 1978, http://www.time.com/time/magazine/article/0,9171,912125,00.html

Powell, Colin. Remarks at the meeting with women's organizations, White House, Nov. 19, 2001.

Richey, Warren. "Sandra Day O'Connor Announces Retirement," *Christian Science Monitor*, July 1, 2005.

Sahadi, Jeanne. "The 76-cent Myth," *Everyday Money*. CNNMoney.com, http://money.cnn.com/2006/02/21/commentary/everyday/sahadi/index.htm

——. "Where Women's Pay Trumps Men's." *Everyday Money*, CNNMoney.com, http://money.cnn.com/2006/02/28/commentary/everyday/sahadi/index.htm

Sellers, Patricia. "Women on Boards (Not!)," *Fortune* at CNNMoney.com, http://money.cnn.com/magazines/fortune/fortune_archive/2007/10/15/100536852/index.htm

Shanahan, Eileen. "Equal Rights Amendment Is Approved by Congress." *New York Times*, March 23, 1972, 1.

Sherman, Mark. "Ginsburg Only Woman on High Court,"
Associated Press, June 4, 2007.
"Some Units of Jaycees Rebel Against Admitting Women."
New York Times, September 10, 1984, A-14.
Soulier, Kate. "Historical Perspective: Does One Vote
Count?" *Earlybird*, no. 13, May 25, 2004. http://www.
utahpolicy.com/pages/newsletters/Issue13.htm
Stanton, Elizabeth Cady. "A Slave's Appeal." Address to
the Judiciary Committee of the New York State legis-
lature, March 1860.
Stanton, E. C., and M. J. Gage. *History of Women's Suffrage*.
Rochester, NY: Fowler and Wells, 1887–1889.
"Suffrage Wins in Senate; Now Goes to States." *New York
Times*, June 5, 1919, 1.
"Tennessee Completes Suffrage Victory." *New York Times*,
August 19, 1920, 1.
"Those Who Sued Jaycees on Bias Celebrate." *New York
Times*, July 5, 1984.
"Woman Suffrage Amendment Wins in Legislature: Unan-
imous Vote Is Given for It in Senate and Assembly."
New York Times, June 17, 1919, 1.
"Women in War Jobs—Rosie the Riveter (1942–1945)."
Historic Campaigns, Ad Council Web site. http://www.
adcouncil.org/default.aspx?id=128
"Women's History in America." Women's International
Center, www.wic.org/misc/history.htm

AUDIO/VIDEO
Niki Caro, director. *North Country*, Warner Brothers, 2005
(movie).

BOOKS AND REPORTS
Archer, Jules. *Breaking Barriers: The Feminist Revolution
from Susan B. Anthony to Margaret Sanger to Betty
Friedan*. New York: Viking, 1991.

Carabillo, Toni, et al., eds. *Feminist Chronicles: 1953–1993.* Los Angeles: Women's Graphics, 1993.

Davis, Flora. *Moving the Mountain: The Women's Movement in America Since 1960.* New York: Simon & Schuster, 1991.

O'Connor, Sandra Day. *The Majesty of the Law.* New York: Random House, 2003.

"Supreme Court of the United States" (booklet). Washington, DC: Public Information Office, Supreme Court of the United States, 1979.

COURT CASES

Adarand Constructors v. Pena, 515 U.S. 200 (1995).

Board of Directors of Rotary International v. Rotary Club of Duarte, 481 U.S. 537 (1987).

Boy Scouts of America v. Dale, 530 U.S. 640 (2000).

Bradwell v. State of Illinois, 83 U.S. 130 (1873).

Brown v. Board of Education, 347 U.S. 483 (1954).

Frontiero v. Richardson, 411 U.S. 677 (1973).

Goesaert v. Cleary, 335 U.S. 464 (1948).

International Union v. Johnson Controls Inc., 499 U.S. 187 (1991).

Lois E. Jenson et al v. Eveleth Taconite Company, U.S. Court of Appeals for the Eighth Circuit, No., 97-1147, filed December 5, 1997.

Minor v. Happersett, 88 U.S. 162 (1875).

Muller v. Oregon, 208 U.S. 412 (1908).

NAACP v. Alabama ex rel. Patterson, 357 U.S. 449 (1958).

New York State Club Association v. City of New York, 487 U.S. 1 (1988).

New York Times v. United States, 403 U.S. 713 (1971).

Personnel Administrator of Massachusetts v. Feeney, 442 U.S. 256 (1979).

Phillips v. Martin Marietta Corp., 400 U.S. 542 (1971).

Railway Mail Ass'n v. Corsi, 326 U.S. 88 (1945).

Reed v. Reed, 404 U.S. 71 (1971).

Roberts v. *United States Jaycees*, 468 U.S. 609 (1984),
    (formerly known as *Gomez-Bethke* v. *U.S. Jaycees*).
Roe v. *Wade*, 410 U.S. 113 (1973).
St. Mary's Honor Center v. *Hicks*, 509 U.S. 502 (1993).
Taylor v. *Louisiana*, 419 US 522 (1975).
U.S. Jaycees v. *McClure*, 305 N. W. 2d 764 (1981).
U.S. Power Squadrons v. *State Human Rights Appeals Board*,
    59 N.Y.2d 401, 410–11, 452 N.E.2d 1199, 1203, 465
    N.Y.S.2d 871, 875 (1983).
United States v. *Virginia*, 518 U.S. 515 (1996).

Documents

Declaration of Sentiments (from Stanton, E. C., *A History of Woman Suffrage*, vol. 1, Rochester, NY: Fowler and Wells, 1889), 70–71), http://www. rochester.edu/SBA/declare.html

Web Sites

Administrative Office of the U.S. Courts.
http://www.uscourts.gov

Cornell University Law School Supreme Court collection.
http://www.law.cornell.edu/supct/

FindLaw (U.S. Supreme Court Cases).
http://www.findlaw.com/casecode/supreme.html

First Amendment Center
http://www.firstamendmentcenter.org

Iowa Court Information System.
http://www.judicial.state.ia.us/students/6

Landmark Cases of the U.S. Supreme Court.
http://www.landmarkcases.org

Legal Information Institute, Cornell Law School.
http://www.law.cornell.edu

Library of Congress, American Memory section.
http://memory.loc.gov/ammem/collections/continental

National Archives, original documents.
http://www.archives.gov

Oyez Project, U.S. Supreme Court multimedia site.
http://www.oyez.org

Sexual Harassment Support Group
http://www.sexualharassmentsupport.org

Supreme Court Historical Society.
http://www.supremecourthistory.org

Supreme Court of the United States.
http://www.supremecourtus.gov

All Web sites accessible as of October 12, 2007.

index

Page numbers in **boldface** are illustrations, tables, and charts.

ABOUT THE AUTHOR

SUSAN DUDLEY GOLD has worked as a reporter for a daily newspaper, managing editor of two statewide business magazines, and freelance writer for several regional publications. She has written more than forty books for middle-school and high-school students on a variety of topics, including American history, health issues, law, and space.

Gold's *The Panama Canal Transfer: Controversy at the Crossroads* won first place in the nonfiction juvenile book category in the National Federation of Press Women's communications contest. Her book, *Sickle Cell Disease*, was named Best Book (science) by the Society of School Librarians International, as well as earning placement on Appraisal's top ten "Best Books" list. The American Association for the Advancement of Science honored another of her books, *Asthma*, as one of its "Best Books for Children." She has written several titles in the Supreme Court Milestones series for Marshall Cavendish.

In 2001 Gold received a Jefferson Award for community service in recognition of her work with a support group for people with chronic pain, which she founded in 1993. She and her husband, John Gold, own and operate a Web design and publishing business in Maine. They have one son, Samuel.